CW00664129

BUSES
YEARBOOK 2005

Edited by STEWART J. BROWN

Ian Allan
PUBLISHING

BUSES

YEARBOOK 2005

First published 2004

ISBN 0 7110 2997 0

© Ian Allan Publishing Ltd 2004

Published by Ian Allan Publishing

an imprint of Ian Allan Publishing Ltd, Hersham, Surrey KT12 4RG.
Printed by Ian Allan Printing Ltd, Hersham, Surrey KT12 4RG.

Code: 0408/E3

Front cover:
Modern high-capacity double-deckers are not restricted to big urban fleets. This Volvo B7TL with Wrightbus Eclipse Gemini body is operated by Reliance Motor Services of Sutton-on-the-Forest, near York. It is a 74-seater and started life as a demonstrator. *Stewart J. Brown*

Back cover:
Fylde Borough Transport put the first Optare Excels into service in the summer of 1996. Fylde was by then owned by Blackpool Transport, and the Excels were painted in Blackpool's Handybus livery, which had previously been applied only to minibuses. *Stephen Morris*

Title page:
When a Megadekka became a MegaDecker. One of Stagecoach's coach-seated Olympian tri-axles in Glasgow, where they operated briefly on a commuter service to Cumbernauld New Town, They subsequently joined the Megabus.com fleet and ran the original Oxford route before the first ex-Citybus Olympians were ready. *Stewart J. Brown*

Contents

DOUBLE-DECKERS *WITH SIX APPEAL*

Alan Millar considers the appeal of buses with six wheels.

I hesitate to use the words 'sex appeal' in the context of buses. It's the sort of phrase that confirms people's worst suspicions about our interest in street-running public transport, so please understand that I'm writing them in a purely platonic context. My point is that if double-deckers possess more of said appeal than single-deckers — and the jury may still be out on where articulated single-decks fit into such emotional rating — then double-deckers with six or more wheels have it in spades.

Those extra wheels may account for some of the posthumous following enjoyed by the British trolleybus, more than 30 years after its demise. Sure, they had other virtues, like near-silent running and unmatched acceleration, but there was something impressive about the girth of a 'Q1' in action to make you feel that here was a bus of substance. In a quite different way, the Bedford VAL

coach caught the public imagination in the early-1960s, its twin-steer layout conveying a futuristic image of travel in the new motorway age. It was a real-life representation of Lady Penelope's pink Rolls-Royce on *Thunderbirds*.

I've never really understood why six-wheel trolleybuses were so much more successful than their motor-bus counterparts, but it is well chronicled that the VAL's extra axle was its downfall. Its Achilles Wheels, as the Greeks most definitely wouldn't have said. Tyre scrub and brake wear were greater than on more conventional chassis, and it died out after about 10 years on the market. We could quite justifiably have assumed that this was an idea whose time had gone.

Yet new British-built tri-axle double-deckers were back on our roads from 1982, and imported ones had appeared here a year earlier. The first of these

Right: **There is something especially impressive about a six-wheel trolleybus. This is one of Newcastle's Metro-Cammell-bodied BUTs, built largely to London Transport's 'Q1' design.** *Ian Allan Library*

Above: **Like Lady Penelope's Rolls-Royce? The Bedford VAL was a symbol of the motorway age. This 1963 publicity shot shows an early example with equally striking Duple Vega Major body.** *Ian Allan Library*

Left: **The Bedford VAL made a distinctive — and rare — bus. North Western bought a batch of Strachans-bodied VAL14s with arched roofs enabling them to negotiate a low canal bridge. The small wheels meant the whole bus could be built low.** *Reg Wilson*

were products of the initial rush to deregulate express coach services in October 1980. Two of the companies that took early advantage of the new regime to challenge National Express and the Scottish Bus Group were Trathens of Plymouth and GT Coaches of Perth. Both started out using single-deck coaches but recognised that they could do better using higher-capacity double-deckers. They had to look to Europe for suitable vehicles and hit on two models that could be adapted for UK operation — the Neoplan Skyliner from Germany and the Van Hool Astromega from Belgium. Both were available with Mercedes-Benz engines and both had a third axle to comply with gross weight restrictions. Oh, and in case you've already started asking 'GT who?', the young proprietors of the Perth company soon changed its name to Stagecoach. Unless you've been living under a stone for the past 25 years, I suspect you'll

recognise that name. It's a business that has had tri-axle double-deckers ever since.

Whether running on Trathens' routes to the West Country or on Stagecoach's between Aberdeen and London, the tri-axle double-deck coaches cut an impressive dash. They reinforced their provision of a different quality of service than had been on offer from state-owned rivals. And, in the case of Trathens, they were soon running in its rival's colours, as National Express recognised the value of co-operating rather than competing.

NatEx — and its parent National Bus Company — also realised that it might like a few tri-axle double-deckers of its own to provide additional services. Being state-owned, its hands were tied more tightly than those Devonian and Scottish upstarts. To explain, I recall reading a wittily written account of the British aviation industry that spoke of a committee set up to decide what sort of airliners our state carriers should buy after World War 2. This account said the obvious answer was 'American ones', but they designed British ones instead. In much the same way, the answer to what NBC (and

SBG) should buy when they needed double-deck coaches was 'German ones'. The Belgian equivalent was nowhere nearly so well regarded as the Skyliner and nothing was available from a British manufacturer. But publicly owned bus companies laid themselves open to accusations of absent patriotism if they invested in imported vehicles. NBC needed its equivalent of the Bristol Brabazon.

The prize went to Metro-Cammell-Weymann, which — like the other UK-based manufacturers — produced tri-axle double-deckers for Hong Kong. For the Far East, it built a jumbo version of the Metrobus, and for this new UK market it developed the Metroliner. In essence this was a Metrobus re-skinned as a coach with lots of curved and bonded glazing and powered for motorway running with a 290hp Cummins L10 engine. When it first appeared in 1982, this was one of the first applications of any sort for the 10-litre Cummins diesel.

While the Skyliner and Astromega were just 4m high to comply with European height limits, the Metroliner was 4.2m high. That's because it was based on a 'proper' UK double-decker, and the good thing was that it had more interior circulating-space than its Continental rivals. You could walk past the front wheels without impersonating Quasimodo in the bell tower at Notre Dame. The less good thing for MCW was that this restricted the Metroliner's appeal to operators running domestic services. No chance of taking one on the motorways of Europe, where many UK operators were using their imported double-deckers. Its other drawback was that the transverse engine (carried over from the

Above: **Stagecoach's long obsession with six-wheel double-deckers began with a pair of Neoplan Skyliners bought for its Aberdeen–Glasgow–London route, one of which is seen in Glasgow when new.** *David G. Wilson*

Below: **ML1, the first tri-axle MCW Metrobus for China Motor Bus, on test in the UK in March 1981.** *Adrian Pearson*

Metrobus) didn't stay as cool at high speed as an in-line unit in a Skyliner.

Reliability wasn't the Metroliner's middle name, and this became a bigger issue as NBC was privatised and its successors faced up to the real costs of running these coaches. Towards the end MCW developed a Metroliner that should have answered those criticisms. The 400GT was 4m high

Above: **Two of NBC's MCW Metroliners load in Coventry in August 1984. The coach on the left is with Shamrock & Rambler, while that on the right is on the Great Yarmouth route operated by Midland Red Express.**
T. W. Moore

Above: **One of the rare 4m-high MCW Metroliner 400GTs, on the London Liner motorway express service operated by West Midlands Travel.**
Adrian Pearson

Right: **Second life for a Metroliner: a former Shamrock & Rambler example converted as an open-top London Pride sightseeing bus.**
Ross Newman

but by then had displayed a long-term interest in the potential of the tri-axle double-decker. A persistent Leyland salesman had shown great faith in the Perth entrepreneurs from their early days and was keen to help realise Brian Souter's dream of using high-capacity double-deck buses. Back in those early days, high capacity was a 78-seat, 31ft-long ex-SBG Bristol Lodekka, but Leyland was building tri-axle 12m Olympians for Hong Kong and was happy to develop a UK version once Stagecoach began buying up ex-NBC bus companies.

Three were delivered in 1988/9, all with low-height Alexander bodies. They formed part of a larger order for similar 10m two-axle buses. Two were kitted out as 96-seat semi-coaches and were used by the Cumberland subsidiary to carry employees from the Sellafield nuclear complex. The one that attracted the most attention was the bus now identified in Stagecoach's national fleetnumbering as 14000, a 110-seat bus. Although it has now spent longer with United Counties, it started out in the Magicbus fleet in Glasgow and was known originally as the Megadekka. Who says young Souter wasn't a bit of an enthusiast for his old Bristols? It also was publicised as Britain's biggest bus.

Maybe the Megadekka had more publicity appeal than practical value back then, but it made clear the company's interest in running the bus equivalent of a jumbo jet. And this was an enthusiasm that didn't diminish. When it expanded into Africa Stagecoach bought 20 Duple Metsec-bodied Dennis Dragon 115-seaters for its Kenya fleet and 10 108-seaters for its Malawi business's inter-city routes. Its short-lived move into Sweden in 1996 saw the Swebus

and had an in-line engine. Sadly, that engine was the new Gardner 6LYT, which never had much chance to develop, and only three had been built when production ended in 1987. In all there were just 130 Metroliner double-deckers — all for public-sector customers. Their new private-sector owners soon sold most of them, although several enjoyed a new lease of life on work that proved less taxing for them. These became open-top sightseeing buses in London, where their ability to carry 63 top-deck passengers outweighed any mechanical problems. In any event, sightseeing buses poodle around at a snail's pace by comparison with the thrashing expected of a motorway coach.

Operators that still wanted double-deck motorway coaches — and Trathens was one of the few that did — stuck mainly with the trusty Skyliner, or for a time with either the Volvo B12T or DAF SBR3000. Not that there were many, as most judged that they were better-off using single-deck coaches.

Stagecoach sold its original express coach business to the privatised National Express in 1989

Above: **An early Plaxton Paramount 4000-bodied Neoplan of National Travel (East) arriving in Leeds on a London–Bradford service. The badge on the front shows that it had a Gardner 6LYT engine.** *K. Watson*

Right: **In its early days as a privatised business National Express identified the visual appeal of the Neoplan Skyliner and commissioned this Skyliner-shaped hot-air balloon, given aircraft registration G-BUSS.** *Ian Allan Library*

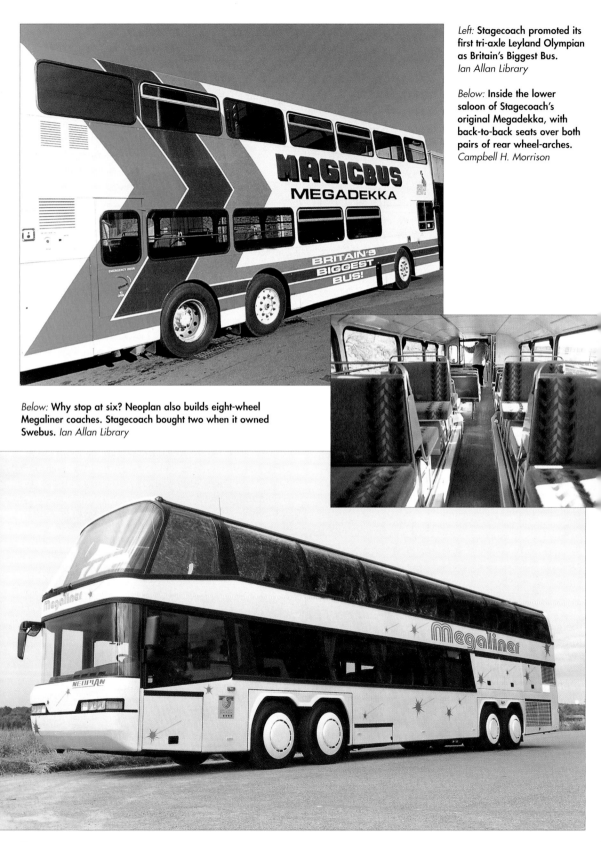

Left: **Stagecoach promoted its first tri-axle Leyland Olympian as Britain's Biggest Bus.** *Ian Allan Library*

Below: **Inside the lower saloon of Stagecoach's original Megadekka, with back-to-back seats over both pairs of rear wheel-arches.** *Campbell H. Morrison*

Below: Why stop at six? Neoplan also builds eight-wheel Megaliner coaches. Stagecoach bought two when it owned Swebus. *Ian Allan Library*

company develop inter-city express services and the addition of its ultimate in high-capacity double-deckers — two 15m four-axle Neoplan Megaliners. Their like has yet to be seen in Britain, but the spirit of the 1981 Skyliners was alive and well.

Stagecoach sold the Malawi business in 1997, and the Kenya business went the following year, but a side-effect of the latter deal was that Kenya's 11m Dragons — which had performed poorly at high altitudes — were shipped to a UK city where the conditions were far less tropical. Manchester, noted (mainly by people who have never set foot in the place) for an apparently wet climate, would become their new home after a major refit.

To comply with European emission regulations, 215hp L10s replaced the Dragons' Gardner engines. Conventional two-abreast seats for a mere 88 replaced their 3+2 seating and they were equipped with heaters; in Africa the only heating issue had been with the engines, which couldn't stay cool at altitudes. Two other features survived the process: they kept their ZF gearboxes (otherwise quite similar four-wheel UK Dennis Dominators have Voith 'boxes) and their deep tropical sliding windows, albeit screwed shut.

And why Manchester? The company had successfully established its low-fare Magic Bus brand on some of the city's contested corridors, where a large student population — one of the largest concentrations in Europe — was happy to pay less for frequent travel. The 88-seat Dragons were ideal for shifting crowds.

Stagecoach also bought itself some brand-new tri-axle double-deckers in 1999 for its Oxford Tube coach service to/from London. Traffic was growing

steadily on this corridor and, rather than again increase frequencies, it got back to the roots of what the original Scottish express company had done in 1981, buying 28 12m MAN 24.350s with 68-seat Jonckheere Monaco bodies. MAN was its favoured chassis supplier at the time, and these vehicles carried a livery that managed to combine Oxford Tube red with the group's familiar orange, blue and red stripes.

The Oxford Tube was a unique service, but Stagecoach's efforts with its Dragons may also have alerted others to the idea of repatriating surplus British-built double-deckers from tropical climes. Singapore Bus Services was interested in selling some relatively modern Volvo Olympians with Alexander Royale bodies, and FirstGroup shipped a five-year-old into its Potteries fleet in 1999 with a view to buying more for school contracts that had a low age limit. These were conventional two-axle buses with equally conventional ventilation; their lack of air-conditioning was one reason for their sale. But the Potteries purchase prompted the import of 10 tri-axle Leyland Olympians from another Far Eastern fleet during 2000.

First had a 24% stake in New World First Bus, a new Hong Kong operator set up in 1998 to take over much of the work of the long-established China Motor Bus company. The new concern was investing heavily in low-floor, air-conditioned buses and was offloading some otherwise perfectly serviceable, high-capacity tri-axle double-deckers that lacked those two key features.

The 10 Olympians were 11m dual-door 109-seaters built in 1993 and fitted with Alexander R type bodies, Cummins L10 engines and ZF

Above: **Two of the 28 Jonckheere Monaco-bodied MAN 24.350s that Stagecoach bought for the high-frequency Oxford Tube. They were due to be cascaded to Scotland after their Neoplan replacements arrived.** *Alan Millar*

Below: **After an initial spell in Greater Manchester, First's 10 Alexander-bodied tri-axle Leyland Olympians settled in Glasgow, where they formed an LT class within the local fleet. They retain tropical guttering above their upper-deck side windows.** *Stewart J. Brown*

gearboxes. They were among the last Leyland Olympians built and were CMB's newest non-air-conditioned double-deckers. Potteries got these too and had them rebuilt as single-door 84-seaters with conventional UK glazing with shallow top-sliders, but retaining the tropical rain gutters on the upper deck. Their new seating capacity hardly matched their length, and half of the downstairs seats faced inwards, as in a London tube train. While they had bench seats over their rear axles, the Stagecoach Dragons had two pairs of back-to-back seats.

Potteries put all 11 of its Far Eastern Olympians into the Pennine unit at Dukinfield, where they operated on Greater Manchester PTE schools services, but all these buses were transferred in 2002/3 to First Glasgow — by then First's tri-axle city.

NWFB had also inherited an even larger collection of 12m tri-axle Metrobuses and Dennis Condors from CMB and these, too, were surplus to requirements. If the Dragon is essentially a tri-axle Dominator, the Condor is — well — just a Dragon

Right: **When is a Dragon not a Dragon? When it's a Dennis Condor built for China Motor Bus. This one, with Wiltshire operator Kinch's of Minety, boasts 106 seats for school transport and was originally a DL-class member of the CMB fleet. Pairs of horizontal handrails prevent its occupants from falling through the tropical sliding windows.** *Dave Rogers*

Below: **A former New World First Bus tri-axle Metrobus with Top Line Travel of York, which was using it for school transport and for registered local bus services.** *Steve Owbridge*

Above: **The low height and long rear overhangs of First Glasgow's 10 East Lancs Nordic-bodied Volvo B7Ls add to the apparent length of these vehicles. Logos either side of the destination box advertise their air-conditioning.** *Stewart J. Brown*

by a different name. The Dragon had first been supplied to the rival Kowloon Motor Bus, but CMB's Peruvian-Chinese managing director insisted that his had to be named after a bird, so they — and only they — honoured one of South America's largest.

There was no chance of First bringing these into UK fleets that were keener to get shot of the Metrobuses and Dominators they already had, but another UK business spotted their potential. Ensignbus, the Essex dealer that made its fortune from selling most of London Transport's DMS Fleetlines, took a chance, importing 40 1987/8 Metrobuses (with Gardner 6LXCT engines) and following these with even more Duple Metsec-bodied Condors. It identified two potential markets for them: one was to take their tops off and use them as sightseeing buses with 61 seats upstairs; the other was as school buses, with something close to their original 110-seat layout. It took a while for the idea to catch on, but Arriva and the Big Bus Company each have nine of the Metrobuses on London sightseeing tours, and Big Bus also has 43 Condors. Several smaller operators use one or both types as school buses, each doing the work of two single-deckers, even if other operators quake at the idea of so many children in one confined space.

Another school-bus operator, MASS Transit, imported 18 of its own tri-axle double-deckers from Hong Kong in 2004 and converted them into 122-seaters for its contracts in South Yorkshire. There were 11 Alexander-bodied Leyland Olympians (all 12m) and seven Duple Metsec-bodied Dragons (five

12m, two 11m), all from Kowloon.

While all this was going on there was a further twist to the tri-axle tale when Volvo and East Lancs teamed up to build 36 three-door double-deckers to the specifications of HT, the Copenhagen transport authority. The Danes were less than enamoured of articulated buses and were persuaded to go for a more British solution with 76 seats, two staircases, air-conditioning and a 12m B7L chassis. They went to two of HT's contractors, City Trafik (which is part-owned by French operator Kéolis) and Arriva, which we all know is British and knows a thing or two about double-deckers.

Unfortunately, Danes didn't take too well to double-deckers and it seems unlikely that there will be any more, although the 4.1m-high East Lancs body — known appropriately as the Nordic — sells quite well overseas as an open-topper on two-axle B7L chassis. However, the complete, roofed package caught the eye of one of First's bright young men. Mark Savelli, who had worked in Hong Kong and helped set up NWFB, was back in Britain in charge of First's Scottish companies and saw potential for a radically different type of double-decker to handle growing numbers of aspirational passengers. He didn't need three doors or two staircases, although I suspect that he (but not his engineering staff) would have preferred two doors. But he did like the idea of an eye-catching, high-capacity double-decker with air-conditioning and persuaded First to let him buy 10 for the Glasgow fleet, with 95 seats and one door. They arrived at the end of 2002, just as Mark Savelli was about to return to Hong Kong to take up a top position at NWFB, in which First by then no longer had a financial interest. The buses have remained in Glasgow, joined by the 10 tri-axle Olympians, but may well turn out to be the only such vehicles in the UK.

Stagecoach also was active in Hong Kong. It ran up to 11 buses (six of them tri-axle Olympians) in a small-scale venture that lasted from 1992 to 1996, but from 1999 to 2003 it owned Citybus, one of the former colony's largest bus fleets. Shortly before selling Citybus it shipped five 1990 tri-axle Olympians with air-conditioned 94-seat Alexander bodies to the UK and followed these a year later with another nine. Like the Magic Bus vehicles, these were painted all-blue, but this time for its new Megabus.com services, offering cheap inter-city travel with on-line booking, aimed primarily at students.

Megabus also became the new home for some of the Manchester Dragons, refitted with coach seating for 92 passengers — more than in their previous short-haul role. The two Sellafield Megadekkas had been moved around too, first onto Magic Bus routes in Manchester, then to Glasgow for a commuter service branded MegaDecker by someone at Stagecoach who clearly didn't know his old Bristols as well as his boss. They moved temporarily to Oxford for the first Megabus service, before settling again in Scotland on the web-booked services there.

If Megabus takes off it seems likely that more tri-axle Olympians will be bought from Hong Kong to provide additional services — proof indeed that one of Britain's biggest bus operators has found a continuing role for tri-axle double-deckers for 23 of its 24 years. And that may not be the end of the story, either, for continued growth of the Oxford Tube has apparently led to an order for 25 13.7m Neoplan Skyliners, with nearly as many top-deck seats as there are on both decks of the MANs. The spirit of 1981 is alive and well.

Be careful where you say it, but you might even consider that these are coaches with sex appeal ...

Below: **A Former Hong Kong Citybus Leyland Olympian in Oxford on the original Stagecoach Megabus.com route from London. Its highbridge Alexander body has coach seats and air-conditioning.** *Alan Millar*

THE
INTERREGNUM

Deregulation brought new colour to Britain's buses in the late 1980s as the National Bus Company was privatised, with new owners and new liveries for buses which had once been either poppy red or leaf green. Then, in the late 1990s, industry consolidation brought new corporate identities. *Stewart J. Brown* illustrates some former NBC fleets in the period before the new corporate looks took over.

Left: Midland Red East reinvented itself as Midland Fox, with a bright red and yellow livery and a stylised fox logo. This MCW Metrobus in Leicester was new to South Yorkshire PTE. The business is now part of Arriva.

Right: Midland Red North tried to recall the heyday of the Midland Red company with an all-over red livery and a traditional-style MIDLAND fleetname. The effect was drab, even on a bright sunny day, as shown by this former Green Line Leyland Tiger coach, which had been given a new lease of life with an East Lancs bus body.

Right: **A bright new look, retaining the old-style fleetname, brought fresh zest to Midland Red North. This is a 1994 Scania with an East Lancs body, seen when new. Like Midland Fox, Midland Red North is now part of Arriva.**

Below: **Midland Red West adopted a red-and-cream livery. As part of the Badgerline group it received Dennis Lances with Plaxton Verde bodywork, one of which is seen in Alcester after Badgerline had joined forces with GRT to form FirstGroup. The red and cream has been replaced by FirstGroup's corporate colours.**

Bottom: **After privatisation East Kent reverted to maroon and cream, the company's colours in pre-NBC days. This MCW Metrobus and the Minilink-liveried Iveco behind it carry logos for the company's 75th anniversary, celebrated in 1990. Today Stagecoach livery rules the routes once served by East Kent's maroon buses.**

Right: Badgerline was a new company created in 1986 to take over the rural operations of Bristol Omnibus. It soon became a major player in the industry, and as its operations spread so did its smiley badger livery, which initially featured these creatures above the side windows. This is a Plaxton-bodied Dennis Dart in Bath.

Left: Cumberland Motor Services was formed in 1986 to take over the northern part of Ribble's territory. Eventually both Ribble and Cumberland would become Stagecoach subsidiaries. This Cumberland Leyland National in Ambleside in 1991 is in Ribble's attractive post-1986 livery, which retained NBC's poppy red but with grey, white and yellow relief.

Right: Northumbia Motor Services, now part of Arriva, was another 1986 creation, taking over a large part of the territory of United Auto. The company adopted a distinctive red and grey livery which took little account of the basic lines of the vehicle. This is an Optare MetroRider.

Above: North Western, taking over Ribble's southern services in 1986, originally used a red and blue livery with diagonal colour breaks, which was designed by the same agency that produced Northumbria's colour scheme. This was later replaced by a brighter livery of red, yellow and blue, as seen on an East Lancs-bodied Dennis Falcon in Manchester. Bee Line was an operation acquired by North Western. Today the company is part of Arriva.

Below: Tees & District was another new business created with the splitting of United Auto in 1986. It adopted a livery of red, yellow and white, carried here on a former NBC Leyland National 2 seen in 1991. This is now an Arriva company.

Top: **Kentish Bus was the southeastern segment of the former NBC London Country business. In 1996 it added new low-floor Scanias to its fleet for operation on the Gravesend–Dartford service. These had stylish Wright Axcess-Ultralow bodies. Once a British Bus operation, Kentish Bus is now part of Arriva.**

Above: **London Country (South West) is also now an Arriva business. In 1989, while part of Drawlane, it was purchasing East Lancs-bodied Dennis buses, including this Falcon, seen in Dennis's home town of Guildford.**

Right: United Counties adopted a dark-green livery in place of NBC's leaf green and added a flash of relief in orange, yellow and cream. This is a late Mk 1 Leyland National. United Counties was bought by Stagecoach, and this livery was short-lived, being replaced by the Scottish-based group's corporate white-with-stripes scheme.

Left: Luton & District, set up in 1986, was formerly part of United Counties. Its first livery, seen on a 1980 Bristol VRT, was red and cream and a considerable improvement on NBC's drab green. Twenty years earlier Luton had been served by red corporation buses. Luton & District is now part of Arriva.

Right: Bus services in High Wycombe were for a time operated by the Wycombe Bus Company, a subsidiary of City of Oxford. New vehicles for the Wycombe fleet included low-floor Dennis Darts with Plaxton Pointer bodies. Services in High Wycombe are now provided by Arriva The Shires.

Right: Rhondda was an old name which was revived after the failure of National Welsh. This Leyland National 2 in Cardiff was new to Bristol Omnibus. The Rhondda business was later bought by Stagecoach.

Left: Tiverton & District was a name used for North Devon (Red Bus) operations around the town after the business was privatised. This is a Wright-bodied Dennis Dart. Along with Southern National, North Devon would be later taken over by FirstGroup, although most services in the Tiverton area are now provided by Stagecoach.

Right: South Wales Transport adopted an unusual two-tone green livery after privatisation, and this lasted until the appearance of FirstGroup's corporate colours. Seen in Swansea, home of SWT's headquarters, this 1980 Bristol VRT has a standard NBC-style ECW body.

Above: NBC's last standard double-deck model was the Leyland Olympian with ECW body. Caldaire adopted green and cream as the livery for its West Riding fleet, seen here on a 1985 Olympian in Leeds. Ownership of West Riding passed to British Bus and thence to Arriva.

Below: An unusual type to find in a former NBC fleet was the Optare Vecta, based on an MAN chassis. Crosville Wales — now Arriva Cymru — bought four 42-seat versions in 1995. One is seen in Chester, with route-branding for the 'Seaside and Deeside' Rhyl–Chester service.

WHEN BUSES
WENT TO WAR

World War 2 ended in 1945. *David Wayman* takes us back 60 years and looks at the challenges of wartime bus operation.

For British bus operators, World War 2 started before the declaration made on 3 September 1939. The Government had circulated transport undertakings the previous year, advising them on the need to begin air-raid precautions (ARP). This included planning for the sheltering of passengers during journeys, the building of staff shelters, the protection of fuel supplies, the dispersal of vehicles when not in use and the training of staff in first aid and decontamination. Parts of some transport garages were adapted for use as decontamination centres in anticipation of enemy gas attacks.

Blackout measures were implemented on 1 September 1939, and failure to observe them was a serious offence. Operators treated their vehicles by wholly or partially coating window interiors or interior light bulbs with blue varnish. In some cases amber was used for windows. Within a short time suitable interior lighting masks became available, and window varnish may then have been removed. Some operators fitted the windows of their vehicles with anti-blast netting. Further stipulations regarding vehicles were as follows:

- Extremities (*e.g.* mudguards) to be marked with white edges
- Bulb to be removed from offside headlamp
- Lamp reflectors to be blackened
- Nearside headlamp to be masked with opaque cardboard with 2in aperture and partial blackening of reflector
- Illumination from side and rear lights to be obscured and reduced to 2in opening
- Stop lights to be reduced to 1in diameter
- Rear numberplate and destination indicators not to be illuminated
- Direction indicators (where used) to be reduced to $\frac{1}{8}$in illuminated strip

Above: **But for the war this magnificent 1942 unfrozen bus of prewar appearance would have run by the Firth of Clyde instead of in the fleet of Derbyshire-based Midland General. Pictured here in postwar Nottingham, it was part of an order for all-Leyland Titan TD7s placed by Western SMT and completed to that company's specification, including distinctive destination box and black stanchions. Identical buses from the same batch were allocated to English municipalities — four to Hull, two to Sheffield and one to Sunderland.** *G. H. F. Atkins*

On 22 January 1940 a new type of headlamp mask was introduced. This comprised a hood with apertures and was more effective than the original requirement. A week later the speed limit in built-up areas was reduced from 30 to 20mph during the hours of darkness, clearly due to concern about the incidence of blackout accidents involving pedestrians. In the case of one municipality, during the first seven months of the blackout there were five pedestrian fatalities involving buses and trams, out of a combined fleet total of 130. From October 1940 it became permissible for a masked headlight to be used on a moving vehicle during air-raid alerts, although side-light apertures had to be reduced to 1in diameter. Then, from 15 September 1941, it was allowable to have two masked headlamps, but rear lights had to be dimmed by a sheet of tissue paper or similar. Later there was some relaxation concerning the illumination of destination blinds. (Street objects such as lamp posts, trees, telegraph poles and junction boxes were given white markings.)

There was an obvious need to conserve materials and fuels, particularly those imported and those required to further the war effort. Production and distribution were in the hands of the Ministry of Supply (MoS). Transport organisation and regulation remained the responsibility of the Ministry of Transport (MoT), which was to be amalgamated with the Ministry of Shipping on 9 May 1941 to form the Ministry of War Transport (MoWT), with Sir Cyril W. Hurcomb as its Director General. The Traffic Commissioner in each area was renamed the Regional Transport Commissioner (RTC), reverting in the early-postwar period. Vehicle fuels were among the many items to be rationed. A typical allowance to an urban operator, based on prioritisation of needs, might be about 80% of normal requirements. Operators had the right of appeal to their RTC.

Within days of the outbreak of war operators had to implement service cuts. This generally took the form of lower frequencies, the part-day withdrawal of some services, earlier final journeys at night, the later commencement of Sunday services and the curtailment or suspension of journeys provided only for leisure purposes. Express coach services were greatly reduced or withdrawn, and non-essential private hire travel generally suspended. At the same time, in many areas there was a greater need for transport to carry essential workers.

Even where services were reduced, labour shortages arose due to the immediate calling-up of those transport employees who were in the Territorial Army or the Naval, Army or Air Force reserves. The situation worsened further as men of relevant age (18-42) joined the armed forces. Operators could resolve the situation only by recruiting women to suitable grades, often with some reluctance and delay, and sometimes with strict conditions. For example, the only women eligible to apply in some cases were those within narrow age limits (such as 21-30) who were single, widows 'without encumbrances', or whose husbands were not in full-time employment. Initially, at least, single women and widows were liable to dismissal upon marriage or remarriage.

While bus conducting was regarded as a suitable grade for women, bus driving generally was not. Consequently, some operators trained a proportion of male conductors to drive and then recruited women to fill the vacancies. The same attitude clearly did not apply to women driving trams, and in fact a relatively small number of women did drive buses and trolleybuses during the war. However, they were often confined to single-deckers. A typical municipal operator's starting wage for conductors was about £2 14s 0d (£2.70) a week. Women were paid slightly less than men, it being argued that women cost more to employ on account of their higher average rate of absenteeism, necessitating coverage of their duties by other employees at overtime pay rates.

Left: **Chassis built by the River Brent, body built by the Tyne, and operated halfway between the two on the Trent: this unfrozen 1942 AEC Regent with lowbridge wartime Northern Coachbuilders bodywork, somewhat squarish and squat-looking, was one of two in the fleet of well-known independent Barton Transport. It is seen here in Nottingham after the war. A pair of identical buses went to Western Welsh.** *Roy Marshall*

Some operators took on 'junior conductors' at peak times, often boys of school age, to give bell signals from the platform and thereby free the conductor for fare collecting. Members of the public were urged not to make unnecessary journeys and in any case where possible to avoid peak-time travel. The staffing situation was eased a little from 1 February 1941, when bus driving became a reserved occupation, which carried exemption from military conscription.

The winter of 1939/40 brought further problems in the form of a prolonged spell of extremely cold weather with exceptionally severe blizzards and drifting. In some cases it was not possible for bus services to operate for up to a week or so. That apart, the wider situation was creating a distinctly gloomy outlook for operators. They had become deeply concerned about the probability of further reductions of fuel supplies, caused by the escalation of hostilities leading to increased military fuel requirements, along with the continued loss of American tankerage.

As to vehicles, following the outbreak of war operators had continued to place orders for new buses, and, while all production did not cease immediately, in general it slowed down as manufacturers gave necessary priority to newer orders for military or other war-effort purposes; indeed, many went over to alternative production entirely until near the end of the war. The possibility of a complete suspension of bus manufacturing understandably caused further alarm, as operators clearly could not keep all their time-expired vehicles running indefinitely.

The Acquisition & Disposal of Motor Vehicles Order, 1940 (ADMV), effective from 10 July, prohibited operators from disposing of any mechanically propelled vehicle (not including trolleybuses and tramcars) without a licence. Further regulations were introduced restricting the information conveyed by vehicles, in order to avoid assisting possible enemy parachute invaders. The test was whether a name could be read from the air or from a slow-moving vehicle. It was permissible for destination indicators to show the names of thoroughfares providing they did not reveal the identity of a particular district, military establishment or munitions factory. Municipal operators usually obliterated the name of the undertaking on vehicles.

The blackout made bus conducting (as well as driving) particularly difficult. Full loads and indeed overloads were more frequent, not only at workers' peak times but also often on the last journeys at night. There were problems identifying the

denomination of some coins. Moreover, unscrupulous passengers would sometimes tender foreign currency, reasonably confident that they would get away with it. Some operators issued conductors with small strap-hung torches, but these did not seem to be very effective.

Enemy action brought about extensive damage and destruction to transport vehicles and property, particularly during 1940/1. London, Birmingham, Coventry and Bristol were among the worst affected. In the case of the last two, served respectively by the municipality and a Tilling company, bombing brought about a premature but permanent end to tramway operations. For obvious reasons, details of these events were not publicised at the time. Replacement bus services had to be provided, yet the bus fleets were also depleted, so the only course of action was to hire vehicles.

Even without losses to enemy action, some operators were hard-pressed to cover essential workers' services, while others, usually away from industrial areas, found themselves with a surplus of stock. For this reason there was a considerable degree of hiring of buses between operators. A typical hire charge would be about £25 per month plus 1d (0.42p) per mile. Nearly 500 provincial buses were hired to the London Passenger Transport Board in the autumn of 1940, ostensibly to cover losses by enemy action. Within about six months, however, London was able to hire out some of its own vehicles to other operators in similar circumstances or otherwise in acute need.

Moreover, during the early part of the war the Ministry of Transport commandeered some buses from operators deemed not to require them, to be used by the War Department for military purposes. Such vehicles, typically single-deck and petrol-engined, were usually returned from about the middle of the war, but this may not always have been to their original fleets. Operators converted other buses to ambulances or ARP mobile canteens, and these did not necessarily return to public service. Some operators which would not otherwise have done so purchased used vehicles.

One method of relieving the problems of peak-time passenger traffic was to stagger working hours, these measures being introduced in some areas following discussions between transport managers and local industry representatives. By early 1941, however, the vehicle situation was becoming desperate. New bus building, already at a low ebb, was looking set to dry up completely. A shortage of spare parts was exacerbating the situation. Operators were already placing orders for delivery 'postwar', whenever that might be, and

Above: Bristol's contribution to wartime transport included unfrozen chassis in 1941/2, wartime production resuming in 1944. London Transport received a total of 29 Bristols, the first nine of which were unfrozen K5Gs with Park Royal utility bodies and the rest Duple-bodied K6As. Subsequently the K5Gs, one of which is seen here operating out of Southall garage and with additional half-drop windows fitted, were converted to K6A specification. *Roy Marshall*

some believed that without replacements they might find their fleets unserviceable by 1942.

In February 1941, therefore, meetings took place between the Public Service Transport Association (PSTA), the Municipal Passenger Transport Association and the Omnibus Owners' Association, with a view to submitting proposals to the MoS and MoT. At the same time, the PSTA was asking its members to submit details of their fleets, including the number of new vehicles ordered since the implementation of the ADMV Order the previous July, details of how their maintenance and repair work was carried out during the previous year, and of the stocks of spare parts held. The Association also asked those of its members that were chassis and body builders for information on orders in hand for civilian passenger vehicles, the position regarding the execution of these orders and the number of such vehicles they could complete per month without disturbing war production and if permitted by the MoS. All the information gained was to be submitted to the relevant ministries.

Among the last new buses delivered under what remained of prewar conditions were two all-Crossley Mancunians for Stockport Corporation in May 1941 and, in the following month, three AEC Regents with Roe bodies for Doncaster Corporation and two Eastern Coach Works-bodied Regents for the Western Welsh Omnibus Co. All three types were fully up to prewar standards before the necessary addition of blackout accoutrements.

It was reported in May 1941 that the MoT was 'straining every nerve' to meet demands for new buses and consulting with operators' associations regarding design and production. At the same time,

the MoS began to make steel available to manufacturers, to enable them to produce much-needed spare parts 'to the same extent as pre-war'. Later that month a joint committee of technical representatives of the National Federation of Vehicle Trades and operators' representatives was formed to collaborate with the MoS in creating a standardised design for bus bodywork.

From October 1941 regulations were amended to permit up to 12 standing passengers on conventionally seated buses, providing this number did not exceed half the seating capacity. At that time also, some single-deck buses were altered to unconventional seating, with long seats placed around the perimeter of the saloon. Buses altered in this way were permitted to carry more than the regulation eight standing passengers, on journeys of up to 10 miles on specific services. A typical bus such as a Leyland Lion or Tiger might be altered to contain perimeter seating for 28 or 30, with standing room for a further 28 or 30.

It was known that 'standard wartime' buses would be without many of the refinements expected in peacetime and that construction was planned to minimise the use of materials and labour. Then, ahead of the anticipated time, in mid-November

1941, the first example was introduced and reviewed in the press. It comprised highbridge bodywork built by Park Royal on a Leyland Titan TD7 chassis intended for London Transport. A double-deck body of this design could be built in 1,200 fewer labour hours than normal. Those mentioned below were among more than 30 items in the specification. Some items were changed later, when the situation regarding materials either worsened or improved (writer's remarks italicised in square brackets). There was a corresponding specification for single-deck bodies.

- Seating capacity to be 56 (30/26) in highbridge version and 55 (27/28) in lowbridge.
- Framing to be of oak, ash, mahogany or teak. Longitudinal rails could be of pitch pine. [*In some cases beech was used in framing.*]
- Exterior panelling, including roof, to be of 20-gauge SWG steel, shaped but not beaten.
- No interior side lining panels permitted.
- Upper saloon emergency exit to be panelled and not glazed [*although glazing introduced from about mid-1943*].
- Window glass to be fixed direct to framing.
- Only one half-drop opening window per side per saloon [*although some builders fitted sliding vents for a time*].
- Variable opening ventilators to be fitted to both forward-facing windows at front of upper saloon [*although some builders did not comply for a time*], and a similar ventilator to the nearside front bulkhead window [*fitted to some early examples but few others*].
- Seats to be upholstered in leather or other suitable materials. [*Wooden-slatted seating generally introduced by about mid-1943.*]
- Interior mouldings, cappings, pillars, etc to be finished in natural grain; ceilings in enamel or cellulose.
- Exterior to be given one coat of approved primer then two further coats of approved paint. [*Colours not stipulated. Some operators able to repaint in own standard livery before entry into service.*]
- Regulation white edging to be applied.
- Rear registration number to be painted on the offside vestibule glass.
- An aperture large enough to accommodate any standard type of destination indicator to be provided in the upper saloon front panelling. No rear or side indicators to be fitted [*although some operators were able to specify them at a typical additional cost of about £4 per vehicle*].

The chassis in question was one of about 430, most of them double-deck models, that the MoS had authorised manufacturers to produce only from components set aside or 'frozen' earlier, when other orders were given priority. This gave rise to the description 'unfrozen' buses. Leylands were in the majority, totalling nearly 200, with smaller quantities of AEC, Bristol and Dennis. Some buses ordered originally by one operator were diverted by the MoT to others. A further 90 chassis intended for export were diverted to British operators. Nearly 70 of them were AEC, Leyland or Sunbeam double-deck trolleybuses, and the others Daimler double-deck and single-deck and Tilling-Stevens single-deck motor-bus models. Of all these unfrozen and diverted vehicles, many had bodies of prewar design, while others had standard wartime bodywork. Some diverted vehicles required dispensation to operate, as they were 8ft wide — 6in greater than the British legal maximum. Leigh Corporation, in Lancashire, claimed to have received the first unfrozen bus, an all-Leyland Titan TD7 of prewar design, on 4 October 1941.

Colloquially, if not officially, standard wartime bodywork was referred to as 'utility', a term already applied to various manufactured goods and clothing bearing a special trademark and produced under the control of the MoS in a basic manner, economising on materials and labour. The public generally accepted the degree of self-sacrifice imposed by the rationing of food, clothing, fuels and some household items, on the grounds that it assisted the war effort and was therefore morally right. At this time — and more so after the introduction of wooden-slatted seating — they were experiencing it in bus travel too.

From now and until the end of 1945 operators had to apply to the MoWT for a licence to purchase a vehicle, with the approval of their RTC. They could state their preference of chassis make, but there was no guarantee that this would or could be met. Operators therefore often found themselves having to accept unfamiliar types, hardly facilitating economy of maintenance procedures. One of the difficulties with utility bodies was that in many cases the only timber available was unseasoned, giving rise to the need for much remedial work in later years; in other cases operators scrapped the original wartime bodies and had new ones fitted. Some builders were given dispensation to use steel framing if this was their standard, where the material was available and a switch to timber would hinder production.

Builders producing utility bodies on either unfrozen or other chassis or trolleybuses — or all three — included the following (the first two known to have used metal framing): Alexander, Northern

Counties, Beadle, Bristol, Brush, Duple, Harkness, Park Royal, Pickering, Massey, Northern Coachbuilders, Roe, Strachans, Weymann, Willowbrook. East Lancs produced metal-framed bodies of non-wartime appearance as replacements of original bodies on older chassis during the utility period, as well as bodies on some unfrozen chassis. Cravens also built some 'relaxed utility' metal-framed bodies early postwar.

Although the unfrozen buses were welcome, and their delivery was to continue to the summer of 1942, they were not enough. There was further dismay when the MoWT announced in March 1942 that only 500 new double-deck chassis would appear during that year, built by one manufacturer. This, of course, was Guy Motors of Wolverhampton. From a design prepared six months previously, the first example was ready by the spring of 1942, but the type does not appear to have entered service for some months.

Guy had experience of building cars, lorries and buses going back to 1914, introducing its Arab model in 1933. Production continued until 1940, although from 1936 the company had concentrated chiefly on lorries, many for military use. The new design was based to some extent on the original Arab but later became designated 'Arab I'. It featured the 7-litre Gardner 5LW five-cylinder engine (a minority having the 8.4-litre 6LW), a four-speed sliding-mesh gearbox and was about 18% heavier than the prewar Arab. The rear-axle ratio could be 6.25:1 or 5.6:1. The Arab II, modified and slightly lighter, began to enter service during the summer of 1943. A few early Arabs had bodies of prewar design originally intended for other chassis that were never built.

Meanwhile, in July 1942 a 'wartime' trolleybus chassis had been introduced. Designated the 'W' type and with two axles, it was built by both Sunbeam and Karrier, two concerns that shared the

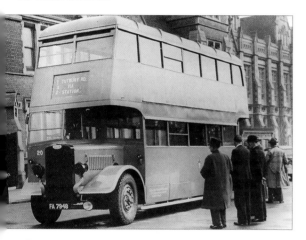

Above: **Seemingly mesmerised by the grey apparition before them, a group of 'admirers' in Burton-upon-Trent focus on a 5LW Guy Arab II, complete with blackout markings and headlamp masks. It shows them the Weymann interpretation of the wartime body design.** *Roy Marshall*

Above right: **South Shields Corporation received among others a trio of 5LW Guy Arab IIs with bodywork by Pickering of Wishaw. Alongside, say, a Massey or Duple product this make of body was quite angular, with little other than the sloping lower edge of the windscreen and the surrounds of the rearmost side window upstairs to eliminate right-angles. This example is seen postwar alongside evidence of enemy action and, although bound for the stadium, was no greyhound itself.** *Roy Marshall*

Right: **Four examples of the Karrier W model with Weymann bodywork were delivered to Ipswich Corporation, the most easterly trolleybus fleet in Britain. These swift, silent vehicles retained their wooden-slatted seating throughout their service careers. Ipswich's destination aperture and layout were unusual.** *Roy Marshall*

same Wolverhampton works. As to traction equipment, there was a choice of British Thomson-Houston, English Electric, General Electric Co and Metropolitan-Vickers, all of about 85hp output. The 56-seat bodywork, initially of Park Royal or Weymann manufacture (Brush was also named, but joined later), was, of course, fully-fronted but otherwise resembled that built on motor-bus chassis. Early examples of the W went to the municipalities of Belfast, Doncaster, Maidstone, Newcastle upon Tyne, Nottingham, Reading, Walsall, Wolverhampton, the South Lancashire and the Mexborough & Swinton companies and Darlington Corporation, the two last-mentioned in single-deck form.

Above: **The Lincolnshire Road Car Co built up a sizeable fleet of Bedford OWBs. This one, an early Mulliner-bodied example, dates from 1942. The nominal seated load of 42cwt (including crew of two) was 64% of the unladen weight (66cwt), compared with the corresponding figure of less than 50% for most utility double-deckers. This made the OWB a highly efficient vehicle as well as one providing a delightful travel experience for those of its passengers prepared to ignore the discomfort of the seating.** *Roy Marshall*

Below right: **Massey Bros' wartime body was dramatic and purposeful, as if to say: "Look, there's a war on, but let's not be timid about our appearance." The deep roof and curved lower edge to the windscreen add to the attractiveness. Early utility products from this builder omitted all the specified upper-saloon forward-facing window vents, and here the operator, Sheffield Transport Department, has increased the number of top-sliding vents.** *Roy Marshall*

The only wartime single-deck motor bus was the Bedford OWB, announced in the autumn of 1942. This 3.5-litre petrol-engined model with four-speed sliding-mesh gearbox, shorter and much lighter than double-deck types, tended to enter service in rural areas or where heavier or larger buses were prohibited or not required. The OWB needed its own body specification and drawing to cater for the

normal-control layout. Thirty-two wooden-slatted seats were stipulated. Duple, Roe, Mulliner and Edinburgh-based operating company SMT built virtually identical bodies on this chassis.

Two important developments occurred during late 1942. The first was an approach by the MoWT to all operators of 150 buses or more, instructing them to convert 10% of their fleets to producer-gas operation. The anthracite-fuelled gas-generating unit was towed behind on a two-wheeled trailer. These contraptions were universally detested: they caused sluggish performance, were dirty, emitted an obnoxious smell, and the trailer created reversing difficulties. These factors often caused operators to confine gas buses to flat routes where reversing at termini was not necessary, but this reduced flexibility of vehicle allocation. Although some operators had already experimented with gas propulsion, with the fuel stored in roof-mounted bags, there was clearly great reluctance to comply with this new requirement, and it seems that many operators may never fully have done so. To the relief of those concerned, the idea was abandoned in September 1944.

The second development was a requirement to cut operated mileage by 10% in order to conserve more fuel and rubber. The loss to Japan of Malaya and other Far Eastern territories had given the enemy control of 90% of the world's natural rubber resources. So precarious was the situation that the MoS would not allow tyres to be renewed unless they were 'worn completely smooth, almost to the canvas'. There was to be no relaxation in the mileage cuts until the following November.

Brighter news before the end of 1942 came in the form of an announcement that Transport Vehicles (Daimler) Ltd was now resuming production, following a halt imposed by enemy action in April 1941. The company had moved from Coventry to temporary premises in Wolverhampton, although this does not appear to have been publicised at the

Right: **This Coventry Corporation utility Duple-bodied Daimler CWA6 is a well-proportioned and restrained design, in contrast to Massey Bros' assertive product. Poor Coventry, nearly blasted off the planet, took delivery of more than 100 unfrozen and wartime-design buses during the 1941-6 period — some 60% of the city's combined tram and double-deck bus fleet total in 1939. Note the wooden-slatted seats and standard fleet livery with blackout additions.** *Roy Marshall*

Below: **Illustrating the lowbridge version of the utility body, in this case built by Roe, a six-cylinder Guy Arab II of 1944 in the SMT fleet sunbathes postwar in Edinburgh's St Andrew Square.** *Roy Marshall*

time. The Daimler CWG5 was the initial model, based on the prewar COG5 although 6cwt heavier. It had the same Gardner 5LW engine, preselective gearbox (in this case four-speed only) and fluid flywheel, along with the option of 5.75:1 or 6.75:1 rear axle ratio. This was good news for those undertakings — mostly municipalities, such as Aberdeen and Dundee — that had tried to standardise on the more easily operated form of transmission prewar.

While only 100 examples of the CWG5 were built, the succeeding CWA6 (with AEC 7.7-litre engine) and later CWD6 (Daimler 8.6-litre) were much more numerous. Aberdeen and Dundee acquired 20 and 16 wartime Daimlers respectively (and no other make) during the 1943-5 period, representing about 48% and 34% of their 1942 double-deck fleet totals.

In 1943 a Daimler CWA6 chassis cost about £1,665, compared with £1,630 for a CWG5, £1,300 for a five-cylinder Guy Arab I and £1,395 for a

Right: **The Brush body was among the more spindly versions of the utility type. This Leeds City Transport example, dating from 1946 and showing the 'relaxed' version of the design with rounded rear roof dome, is seen well into the postwar era, with sliding window vents and a non-original radiator shell.** *John Fozard*

similar Arab II. A typical utility body cost about £910 in the case of Massey, £870 Pickering and £890 Duple. Double-deck chassis prices had risen by about 60% and body prices by about 15% since 1939. The Bedford OWB was originally offered complete at £825. All were to rise further by the end of the war.

With Daimler, Guy and Bedford buses now being produced, along with Karrier/Sunbeam trolleybuses, the anxieties of operators were relieved a little. Then the MoWT announced in September 1943 that production would continue the following year without much variation in the number and types.

By the end of 1943 utility buses were becoming a familiar sight in all operating sectors the length and breadth of Britain. Initially there had been some doubts about the suitability of the Gardner 5LW engine for the majority of Guys, some of which weighed about 7¾ tons unladen. Such a bus would have a nominal power-to-weight ratio of about 0.55bhp/cwt unladen and 0.37 laden, compared with, say, a typical late-prewar 7.7-litre AEC Regent of similar seating capacity but approximately a ton lighter, for which the figures would be about 0.72 and 0.47 respectively. In general, however, the performance of a five-cylinder Guy, while not sparkling, was adequate on moderately undulating terrain, particularly with the 6.25:1 rear axle ratio rather than the optional 5.6:1. Operators were impressed with the fuel economy and reliability of the Gardner and, after a few early minor problems, the rugged nature of the chassis. The similarly-powered and slightly lighter Daimler CWG5, particularly with optional 6.75:1 rear axle ratio and assisted by faster gear changing, gave reasonably good acceleration up to a maximum speed of 30mph. As for the Daimler CWA6, usually a little lighter than the CWG5, for all but the most hilly

terrain the 5.75:1 rear axle ratio was probably the more suitable of the options. There was smart performance from the lively AEC 7.7-litre engine, which, mounted rigidly in this chassis, vibrated heavily and was noisy, although this hardly seemed to matter. ('7.7', incidentally, was a marketing designation, the precise swept volume being 7.58 litres.)

Turning to single-deckers, the Bedford OWB, like the peacetime OB, was a most endearing model and emitted 'fruity' vintage gearbox sounds that almost drowned the resonant hum of the engine. Performance was ample, and the model was reliable and easy to maintain. Legroom between seats, however, was hardly generous.

The operating industry gave two cheers for the announcement made in September 1943 by Ernest Bevin, Minister of Labour & National Service, that oil supplies were better, rubber supplies were going to be better and that more new buses were to be provided. The trade press subsequently implied that bus operation had become the Cinderella of the war effort, clearly not regarding Mr Bevin as the fairy godfather. Tyre supplies were still a cause of anxiety, and the MoS said soberly that expected deliveries of synthetic rubber from the USA would ease the situation only a little.

Gardner engines were still in heavy demand, so, when the Bristol Tramways & Carriage Co was authorised to resume chassis production in the late summer of 1944, it was the AEC 7.7-litre that was installed in the K-type chassis, with four-speed constant mesh gearbox, making it the K6A. The Tilling Group, of which Bristol was a member, particularly seemed to welcome the advent of this model.

During the war, in addition to new vehicle prices mentioned previously, average bus-operating costs nationally had risen by the following approximate percentages: lubricating oil, 80; petrol and fuel oil, 50; materials and spare parts, 40; platform staff wages, 30. Moreover, the manufacturing industry had produced about half a million heavy vehicles, 80,000 light vans and cars, 75,000 carriers and armoured cars and 25,000 tanks; but only 5,000 double-deck buses, some 3,000 single-deckers and about 200 trolleybuses.

In September 1944, after the Allies had broken through the Siegfried Line, liberating Belgium and driving German troops into retreat across Europe, British blackout regulations were relaxed a little. Public transport was permitted to use adequate

lighting again, and subsequently headlamp masks were dispensed with. Supplies of aluminium could now be allocated to the coachbuilding industry for panelling, leading to small weight reductions. In March 1945 the MoS invited applications for licences to purchase Crossley chassis, although these would not appear until 1946.

The later war years brought about unprecedented passenger loadings. For municipalities, averages of some 15 or 16 passengers per bus mile — and more than 20 on trams — were not unusual and hardly likely to be achieved again. But when the war ended in Europe on 8 May 1945 there could be no immediate return to prewar standards of service, and it was to be some months before anything approaching that level could be contemplated. Only now did it seem to be dawning on Britain that transport had played a wartime role more vital than had probably been realised at the time.

Left: **The end of the road. The Northern Counties body on this Dundee Corporation Daimler has had a mid-life rebuild — the flush-mounted glazing is the give-away — but is about to meet the breaker's torch in a Glasgow scrapyard in 1965.** *Stewart J. Brown*

Below: **While some wartime buses were withdrawn from service in the late 1940s and early 1950s, others had remarkably long lives, often after major body rebuilds, as here in Aberdeen, where a Duple-bodied Daimler CWA6 works a lunchtime-peak journey in 1964.** *Stewart J. Brown*

ABROAD
THOUGHTS FROM
HOME

Yes, there is life beyond Calais, suggests *Gavin Booth*, with a look at some more or less familiar types in less familiar places.

All photographs by the author

I t's official. Foreign Buses Are Interesting. Well, maybe not official, but I hope I can convince any borderline xenophobes that foreign buses are worth a second look when you emerge from the plane into 90° heat at some Mediterranean airport looking for the quickest way to your hotel.

Perched on our little island to the west of mainland Europe, we didn't have much truck with foreign buses. We were happy to sell buses overseas, of course, but as the British Empire sank slowly in the west, so did our exports and our bus-building industry. Only the Far Eastern interest in

UK-style double-deckers in the past 30 years has helped to give what's left of the industry a chance to enjoy some serious export sales.

So if you're looking for UK-built buses, head to Hong Kong or Singapore for these big three-axle 'deckers, or to countries like Iceland or Spain to find mirror-image versions of the ubiquitous Dennis Dart.

Ever since Volvo started nibbling at the heels of the UK bus and coach market more than 30 years ago, followed in gradual succession by Bova, DAF, Iveco, MAN, Mercedes-Benz, Neoplan, Scania and all the others, foreign buses and coaches suddenly

Right: Traditional Renaults like this one could be seen in Paris until fairly recently. Pictured in April 1997, it wears the current RATP livery.

Below: British-bodied double-deckers can be seen on open-top services in various cities. This Volvo B10M of L'OpenTour in Paris has East Lancs bodywork.

Left: Sometimes you don't even have to leave your hotel room to photograph buses. Italian coaches pass the author's hotel room in Amalfi in October 1997.

Right: Preserved by the Porto municipality, an AEC Regent V with locally-built UTIC forward-entrance bodywork.

Top: One of Porto's 90 impressive Caetano-bodied Leyland Atlanteans delivered in 1966/7, seen in October 1988.

Above: Pre-booked tickets were required for the Madrid–Toledo express service, which used coaches like this 15m Setra.

seem more familiar. A Volvo B12M with Jonckheere bodywork for a UK customer looks very like one you'll meet on a European autoroute, and the Mercedes-Benz Citaro is probably the closest thing you'll find to a pan-European citybus. Even the characteristics that gave the UK market a certain individuality have gone: look at the spread of articulated buses and the relaxation of the 12m overall length regulation.

But it would nullify my argument that foreign buses are interesting if I pretended that all the buses you will encounter in your overseas travels will look like wrong-way-round UK vehicles. There are some, of course, like the Darts already mentioned, and the Hong Kong and Singapore 'deckers look comfortingly familiar in right-hand-drive layout, but many are as distinctively 'foreign' as ours are distinctively domestic.

The first time I set foot on foreign soil — other than trips across the border from Scotland into England — was a school Cadet Force trip to Northern Ireland that included a day trip over the border to Dundalk in the Irish Republic. What buses I was able to see — splendid veterans from the Violet Bus Service fleet, as well as GNR types — fell into the 'comfortingly familiar' bracket, with just that extra bit of individuality — GNR Gardners, particularly. But it was my second expedition, a day trip to Boulogne, that really introduced me to the difference. And *vive la différence*, as they say.

Above: **A 15m low-floor Neoplan used on the service to Barcelona airport, seen in October 2001.**

Here in Boulogne were buses just as characteristically French as East Kent's AEC Regent Vs at the port of departure were characteristically British. Here were buses that I associated with Paris — Saviems and some unusual buses that only on my return did I identify as Brossels, built by Leyland's Belgian distributor and fitted with Leyland engines at the rear. This was 1969, so rear-engined Leyland single-deckers were still rare in these pre-National days. The Saviems posed a problem, though: where *was* the engine? The answer, following some careful listening, was under the driver — an utterly sensible place, as it allowed a lowish floor from front to back.

So, a fairly painless introduction to foreign buses. But little chance in just a few hours to get to grips with the Boulogne Corporation (yes, I know that's not what it's called) system.

As overseas travel became easier and more affordable, so the destinations for our family holidays were often chosen partly because, somewhere in the back of my mind, I recalled something I'd read that suggested that this area could field some interesting buses — and, indeed, trams. It took my wife and children a few years to work out why we usually seemed to visit places awash with public-transport interest. Even holidays

Above: **And if you want a Dennis Dart, here's a Spanish example operating in Madrid in 2000.**

chosen by the rest of the family for sunshine and beaches would usually yield some unexpected transport attractions.

Now let me get one thing straight. On family holidays I do family things — sitting on the beach, visiting places of interest, enjoying meals together. But the faithful Canon is usually on my shoulder — just in case — and we eschew car hire in favour of local transport. And there is usually one day that is Dad's Day, a day when the family soaks up the sun and I soak up the buses.

It's a bit daunting at first. You see an interesting bus: you have no idea where it's going, how long it takes, how much it costs — even where to buy the ticket. If your language skills stretch no further than Higher French, actually asking someone is a bit of a challenge. I have tried asking holiday-company reps about the local buses, but they look bemused and suggest car hire or coach excursions. Now, excursions can be useful things if you want to travel longer distances; we managed Florence, Rome and Venice from the Adriatic in this way — on different days, it must be said. But for local trips these excursions can be expensive when compared with the cost of making the same trip by public transport.

The Booth way to get information about local transport is to observe. Half an hour at the bus station soon gives you a picture of the transport patterns. If there are interesting buses, are they always on the same route? Do the locals already have tickets, buy them from machines, or pay the driver? Are there timetables and maps you can simply pick from racks, or are they stored behind an enquiry counter manned by staff who are daring you to make a fool of yourself by asking for one. One? One for each route would be great, but why on earth should an obvious visitor need the full set?

If there is bus-stop information, then careful study will point you towards services that give you a reasonable chance to return without hassle. It wouldn't be the first time I had leaped on a bus and hopped out at the suburban terminus to photograph it, only to see it disappear off into the distance. With no timetable information, it's difficult to know how long you will need to wait in 90° heat for the next one. Has the driver just taken it off to the garage for a crew changeover? Who knows? And you're gasping for a cool drink; there are either no shops in sight, or there is the fear that, if there is one, the minute you set off towards it, the next bus will arrive and depart as quickly as its predecessor. Needless to say, it will arrive as soon as you push open the shop door, and so you abandon any thoughts of the cold-drinks cabinet, rush to the terminus and climb aboard. That's when you hear the engine dying as the driver switches off and strolls across to the shop for his cold drink.

You grow in confidence after a few overseas jaunts, but no amount of research can prepare you

Top: Bus preservation is not a purely UK activity. This is a fine Rotterdam Verheul integral incorporating Leyland Royal Tiger mechanical units.

Above: A UK link with the United States is provided by this Stagecoach-owned Coach USA 45ft-long Van Hool integral, seen in Boston in July 2002.

Left: **Elderly trolleybuses could still be found working for the Massachusetts Bay Transportation Authority in Cambridge in July 2002. This is a 1975 Flyer.**

Below: **In July 2002 the Massachusetts Bay Transportation Authority introduced its first BRT (Bus Rapid Transit) line using CNG-powered 40ft City Flyers, as an alternative to a light-rail service.**

Bottom: **This impressive 15m Volvo B10BLE with Carrus body is working for Skånetrafiken in Helsingborg, Sweden — an easy day trip from Copenhagen.**

for the Terminus From Hell. Think of the worst urban terminus in the UK, with packs of dogs and young people roaming the area. Translate it to a country where you're obviously a tourist with an expensive camera and the language is difficult to understand, and you can experience a few anxious moments. My personal anxious moments came at a shanty town in Portugal and a ghetto area in St Louis, USA, when discretion over-ruled valour and no photos were taken; but in daylight in hot weather, the danger was probably more imagined than real.

A less dangerous (if more expensive) way to suss out a new town or city is on a sightseeing tour. With more and more of these on offer, often using old UK buses and sometimes using newer UK-bodied buses, these are invaluable for spotting good photographic locations and provide a useful grandstand for taking interesting shots.

Some countries provide superb transport information, often with good at-stop displays and even staff who speak embarrassingly good English (though they usually let me finish my faltering attempt at their language before answering in English). The Dutch are generally very good at transport, and there is near-seamless transfer from train to bus and from bus to bus throughout the Netherlands. The Swiss and Germans too provide efficient transport with good-quality information, right down to buses that sit at termini with their destination displays counting down electronically the number of minutes before they depart; no cold-drink problems there, then.

If you are intent on a day of bus and tram riding, these days more places offer you day tickets that take the uncertainty out of paying fares and choosing destinations. A pocketful of coin is always useful: the pristine 100-euro note from Thomas Cook doesn't often go down well with drivers, for some reason.

Pre-booking for longer trips is the norm in some countries. In Spain, on services you might expect to pay for as you board, you are often required to buy your ticket at a bus-station office — and be warned: one of the numbers on your ticket is your seat number. Grabbing the front seat to watch the driver is not encouraged if you have been allocated seat 39. Unless you are a fluent Spanish speaker, I wouldn't encourage even attempting to ask to book the front seat. I don't imagine even the old British standby, speaking English slowly and loudly, will cut much ice.

Now you might think that my association with *Classic Bus* magazine would mean that I only look for older buses and turn up my nose at 'modern junk', as some of CB's readers would have it. Not at all. While there are countries like Malta and Portugal where you can still enjoy the buses of yesteryear, in mainland Europe and North America the bus parc is usually fairly young. And with heavily subsidised public transport the buses are often expensive, state-of-the-art machines. The first low-floor buses I ever saw were in the Netherlands — a demonstrator noted working in Amsterdam that I never managed to pin down properly and the first of a fleet of low-floor Neoplans for HTM in The Hague, some years before the UK's first low-floor single-deckers (also Neoplans) entered service.

There *are* old buses, of course, and as in the UK they are often dragged out only at the weekday peaks, so if you're slow off the mark you might

Right: **A Paris-style bus in service in Genova. Like the Paris equivalents it has the engine under the driver, but, being in Italy, it is a Fiat.**

Above: **A self-contained trolleybus system runs along Italy's Adriatic coast between Rimini and Riccione, using Volvo B59 vehicles.**

Below right: **An older Mercedes-Benz artic on the busway in Essen that runs in the centre strip of a busy main road.**

never see them. A tip: if you see something really unusual, photograph it — immediately. The First Law of Finding Buses on Overseas Holidays is that unusual buses will appear only once and you'll never see them again.

The old buses I have traced, sometimes as a result of an early start, include the remnants of the huge Paris fleet of open-rear Renault TN4H, in 1970, and four-axle articulated Fiat trolleybuses in Milan, in 1996. Barcelona provided a tantalising glimpse of an elderly Pegaso artic in 1997, and patient detective work was rewarded with a trip on one of these. Madrid was still home to a fairly large fleet of very Leopard-ish Pegasos in 1999, and in the Netherlands, well into the 1990s, you could still find Leyland chassis under what at first glance were Dutch standard inter-city buses.

Double-deckers, other than tourist vehicles, are increasingly rare outside the UK and the Far East. On my first visit to Paris in 1970 I saw one of RATP's small batch of Berliet double-deckers, looking like standard single-deckers with an upper deck grafted on, which is probably what they were. In Rome in 1976 I was delighted to find, ride and photograph double-deckers, strange beasts to a design that owed little or nothing to their UK counterparts. In New York in 1979 I was able to find a couple of the eight Leyland Atlanteans delivered in 1976, by asking at every public-transport information kiosk I could find; at least the Americans speak a form of English.

Double-deck heaven was Portugal on my first visit

in 1985, with disconcertingly familiar-looking AEC Regent Vs and Daimler Fleetlines with local mirror-image Weymann-ish bodies in Lisbon and distinctively Portuguese Caetano-bodied Atlanteans in Porto. The mirror-image was reversed, so to speak, when HT in Copenhagen took Volvo B7Ls with East Lancs Nordic bodies, and First Glasgow later opted for the right-hand-drive versions. The Copenhagen buses provide a grandstand view of this attractive city.

There are some stunning bus experiences out there in Greater Abroad. Buses that perform hair-raising feats on frankly dangerous roads like the cliff-top road that winds along the coast between Salerno and Amalfi in Italy. And there are buses that help you realise your dreams. In the United States, on business in the Los Angeles area, I was keen to see and walk on the Pacific shore for the first time. We were staying in West Hollywood, and my colleagues were busily hiring cars and taking taxis to travel around. Detective work again, and the realisation that the local Los Angeles Corporation bus linked downtown LA with Santa Monica, on the Pacific coast. For a tiny fraction of the car hire cost, I was able to realise my ambition.

And you do meet the locals that way, sometimes more intimately than you might prefer in a crowded standee bus. In just such a bus, *en route* for the Vatican on a Sunday morning, my son watched with fascination as a pickpocket systematically worked his way towards the rear doors, taking what he could. Discretion, my son had decided, was the sensible answer. Years later I nearly lost my trusty Canon to a suspiciously well-dressed man crushed beside me on the rear platform of a Lisbon tram. But don't let these stories deter you from travelling on overseas buses and trams; just keep an eye on your money, your passport and your camera — not necessarily in that order.

These days there are fewer places where you will find old British vehicles operating in anger rather than on tourist services. Portugal still boasts a dwindling fleet of the AECs that were once almost universal outside the city fleets, but you have to work much harder to find them now. Malta's fleet of British-built buses is also dwindling: new, low-floor buses from China and Turkey are replacing the Maltese veterans at an alarming rate, but you will still see AECs, Bedfords and Bristols, usually heavily rebuilt and declaring themselves to be something other than what at first glance they appear to be.

At the other end of the scale, you can marvel at the latest developments in bus operation in Europe. Sadly, the guided trolleybuses that shared the Essen tramway tunnels no longer do, but I challenge you not to be impressed by two Dutch developments: the double-articulated Van Hools in Utrecht and the frankly amazing 40km Zuidtangent bus link between Haarlem, Hoofdorp, Schiphol airport and southeast Amsterdam — 24km on entirely reserved busway.

And if, after all that, you still feel that Happiness is a Warm Dart, well, you'll even come across some of these in the great undiscovered territory that is Abroad.

Left: Boulogne 1970, and a Belgian-built Brossel BL55 with Jonckheere body. Mechanically, it had a Leyland O.600 engine and Pneumocyclic gearbox.

VR VARIETY

Mention the Bristol VRT and many enthusiasts will think of ECW bodywork and standardised NBC liveries. *Geoff Mills* shows some of the variety to be found among the VR family.

Left: Cumberland Motor Services is connected to Cambridge, where this photograph was taken, by the common ownership (by Stagecoach) of Cumberland and United Counties. This VRT was new to Cumberland in 1980 but is seen operating for United Counties in 1992, still promoting the Workington & Whitehaven Co-op's low prices.

Below: Although looking like a standard NBC VRT, this bus was in fact new in 1978 to the AERE (Atomic Energy Research Establishment) at Harwell. By 1992 it had forsaken the world of atomic research for a more mundane existence as Berry's Beaverbus in Taunton.

Right: **Highbridge ECW bodies on VRTs were uncommon and ungainly. Lincoln City Transport had ten, one of which is seen in Watford in 1992 in the ownership of Luton & District. It is still in Lincoln livery.**

Left: **It's surprising how much a change of grille affects the whole appearance of a familiar design. This VRT in the Ensignbus fleet is fitted with the front panel from an ECW-bodied Bristol LH. New to Western National in 1978, it joined Ensignbus in 1989. The location is the huge Lakeside shopping centre at Thurrock.**

Right: **When it came to bodying VRTs, Northern Counties produced some of its least attractive products. New in 1977 to Cleveland Transit, this example is seen on a park-and-ride service in Chester in 1990, by which time it was owned by local operator Lofty's.**

Above: Only marginally more attractive, and still not up to Northern Counties' usual design standards, were the bodies built on VRTLL chassis for Reading Transport in 1973/4. Two are seen later in life, with Norfolk's of Nayland and Cedric's of Wivenhoe.

Below: MCW bodywork was specified by West Midlands PTE for 45 VRTs delivered in 1976. In 1988 this example was running for Wilts & Dorset in Poole.

Right: **Fareway was one of many small operators to start services in Liverpool after deregulation in 1986. Its original fleet included East Lancs-bodied VRTs purchased from the city's major operator, Merseyside PTE.**

Left: **A few independents bought new VRTs. One was Hutchings & Cornelius of South Petherton, with this 1973 example. It is seen in Swansea in 1982, after sale to West Wales of Tycroes.**

Right: **The Scottish Bus Group was reluctant to let its VRTs travel any distance, and one wonders what its engineers would have made of this former Central SMT bus, one of eight ex-SBG VRTs owned by Top Deck Travel, which specialised in exotic holidays. Russia, Scandinavia and North Africa are among the locations listed on the side — all a far cry from the vehicle's original haunts around Glasgow.**

Right: Most NBC VRTs had ECW bodies, although a small number were bodied by Willowbrook. In 1980 South Yorkshire PTE disposed of 18 eight-year-old East Lancs-bodied VRTs which it had acquired from Sheffield Transport. Maidstone & District took 12, while six went to Crosville.

Left: The bodies fitted by East Lancs to VRTs were generally not among the company's happiest designs. Built in 1981 for Rhymney Valley, this was in fact quite a well-proportioned design, marred only by the oddly styled grille. It was purchased by Beestons of Hadleigh in 1992.

Right: When United Auto took over The Eden it initially retained the independent's fleetname, seen here on a 1977 VRT transferred from the United fleet. The only double-decker to carry 'The Eden' fleetnames, it was photographed at Bishop Auckland in 1996.

Left: This 1976 VRT started life with Western National but by 1999 was in service with Provincial in Portsmouth.

Right: Provincial's bright cream-and-red livery is still carried by this VRT in service with Western National, which had only recently acquired it from the Hampshire company when it was photographed in Plymouth in the summer of 1997. Dual-door ECW-bodied VRTs were relatively rare; this one had been new to Bristol Omnibus in 1980.

Left: In FirstGroup ownership Eastern Counties still had a substantial fleet of Bristol VRTs with standard NBC-style ECW bodies. Less common was this East Lancs-bodied example, which had been new to Northampton Transport in 1982 and is seen with Rosemary Coaches fleetname in King's Lynn in 1998.

Above: In 2003 dealer Ensignbus was looking for export sales for VRTs and converted this one-time Eastern Counties bus to right-hand entrance. The original doorway was panelled over and the door relocated to mid-wheelbase on the offside. It retained right-hand drive.

Below: There can have been few smarter VRTs in service in 2004 than this pair operated by Lodge's of High Easter, Essex. Purchased from Hedingham Omnibuses in the autumn of 2003, that nearer the camera was new to Alder Valley in 1980, while that on the left is a one-time Trent bus.

TEN *MORE* MINUTES

There never seems to be enough time to take the bus photographs we really want, says *Peter Rowlands*, who recounts some of the hazards he's encountered along the way.

All photographs by the author

It has to be a kind of madness. How else can I explain it? I'm cowering under the awning of a shop front in Sunderland, with rainwater splashing up off the pavement and trickling down my neck. It's June 1991, and this is not at all the kind of weather I hoped for at this time of year.

I'm watching a Leyland Olympian of Go-Ahead Northern approaching me — not a bus I particularly came here to see — and wondering how to expose a photograph that will freeze its motion and still have any kind of detail in it.

As it closes on me and starts to make the turn I step out into the deluge and press the shutter, more in desperation than with any confidence. Water sprays out in its wake as it passes, and I see that there are splashes on my lens. Oh well. At least I tried.

What else can you do if you're driven? Driven to take bus photographs whenever you can? The North East is hundreds of miles from my home, and

Above: Torrential rain adds some drama to an otherwise routine picture of an ECW-bodied Leyland Olympian of Go-Ahead Northern at Sunderland in 1991.

Below: An ECW-bodied Bristol RE of East Midland, far from home in a rain-drenched Brentwood in August 1987.

I'm lucky to get here once in two or three years. Glancing at my watch, I see that I have about 10 minutes left before I must go off to the business appointment that brought me here. Ten minutes to flesh out the dream …

Four years earlier, same thing, but this time at Brentwood in Essex — not exactly a Mecca for the bus industry, but given new focus by a remarkable bit of deregulation initiative. East Midland Motor Services, better known for operations around Mansfield in Nottinghamshire, has put on a service out to the east of London, and it's using wonderful veterans such as ECW-bodied Bristol RE single-deckers.

I'm on my way to somewhere else (don't ask me where), but I've diverted here fleetingly to capture this miracle on film. And what do I get? A torrential downpour, the like of which I've never seen. So I pull up against the kerb, shelter in my car and wait for something interesting to come along.

This time I do get buses I actually want — some of the REs, plus other oddments like Leyland Nationals of Eastern National. But the downpour is a serious impediment. Water is backing up from the gutters, sloshing out into the road, drumming on the roof of my car. As soon as I raise the camera the lens is wet and the image is blurred.

Get out, lift camera, take shot, get in again, wipe lens, get out again. Rail against the weather gods.

Presently I check the time, start the engine and pull out from the kerb. I've got to go. And what

happens? The rain slackens, the sky brightens, and I curse. Damn the 10-minute rule.

Rain isn't the only hazard when you're in a rush. Another is simply not knowing where to go. I must have photographed buses in every major city in Britain — and many not-so-major towns as well — and I cherish the notion that I've got all the town centres mapped out in my mind. But actually it's a myth. I arrive at the ring road; I try to think which slip road to take, and where the nearest on-street parking is; but can I remember? Then, when I finally get there, they've demolished half a city block and put in a one-way system, and nothing looks the same any more.

Leicester always gets me that way. I swear they rotate the whole town centre on its axis between my visits — and rebuild all the multi-storey car parks in different streets.

And that's not the only puzzle Leicester poses. What about the Great Crossroads Challenge? There's no lack of interesting buses in Leicester, but when you're in a hurry you're simply spoiled for

Below: **Which way to turn? A Wright-bodied Volvo of FirstGroup heading towards the Charles Street crossroads in Leicester in the summer of 2002.**

Above right: **Sun, pedestrians and other traffic were all kind as this Leyland Olympian of Centrebus arrived at traffic lights in Leicester in the summer of 2002.**

choice. Summer 2002: and, as in so many previous visits, I hover uncertainly at the junction of Charles Street and Humberstone Gate, trying to compute all the variables whilst at the same time monitoring the traffic in four directions at once.

There's the sun — pretty high in July, but better from some angles than others — and there's a cloud that may or may not obscure it in the next minute or so. There's the volume of pedestrians who might block the view. There's the phasing of the traffic lights and the danger that waiting vehicles will stack up in two lanes, with cars in the outer lane blocking the view I want. There's that bus stop a hundred yards down the street; will the buses I want stop there or not?

I could cite plenty of other cities that pose a similar conundrum — Southampton, Portsmouth, Newcastle (the top of Bigg Market), to name but a few.

And there's a question of bus priority — the priority I give to the pictures I want. Do I settle for a nice sunny view of an average bus or hold out for a flawed shot of a much rarer one? It's all too much.

Click: ALX-bodied Volvo of FirstGroup. Click: Alexander-bodied Olympian of Centrebus (or was it a Dominator?). Click: Wright-bodied Barbie bus. Click: nice new East Lancs Lolyne of Arriva. Click: man walking in front of bus (inconsiderate fool). But which vehicles have I photographed so far? Can't remember. Click click.

Let's be honest here: I'm not a professional bus photographer. Are you? I'm not even the kind of hobbyist with whole days to spare on setting up one shot. I'm an opportunist, slotting the endeavour into a busy life. Sure, there are times when I have hours rather than minutes at my disposal, and I'll always make an effort to photograph something worthwhile if I can. But luck inevitably plays a big part.

When I show you the pictures, of course, I'll try to make out that they're exactly what I intended — and imply that I have a whole stock of similar ones back at home. Well, we're all prey to vanity, aren't we?

But let's not short-change ourselves: photographing buses really is quite difficult. Anyone can stand in a busy street and point a camera; but is the bus obscured by traffic or pedestrians? Is it well lit? Does it have hideous reflections in the windows and panelling? Is the driver making an obscene gesture at you? Is it, when all's said, a nice view or an interesting bus?

Fog. Now there's another hazard when time is tight. In fact if I'm passing a town and it's foggy, I probably won't even bother to stop. But if I'm already there it's hard to resist the challenge. And, remarkably, pictures taken in fog can actually have a bit of drama about them — especially if you're near enough to the vehicle to pick out the detail.

Brighton seafront on a foggy afternoon in 1997 might not seem terribly exciting to anyone, but when a Marshall-bodied Dennis Dart of Brighton & Hove comes along, I can't resist the opportunity. Cars' headlights reflect off the streaming pavement; the bus's own headlights add further interest. Click — and the result is passable at least.

In fact in some ways fog is not nearly as bad as the photographer's real enemy on the weather front — cloudy overcast. We've all been there, and seen the results. Over-exposure, to compensate for the dullness, and heavy, over-saturated prints that the photographic shop couldn't be bothered to correct. Three cheers for the digital age — at least we now have the power to put these things right for ourselves. Not so in the past, though, when every overcast print or washed-out slide was a silent reproof to us for trying against the odds.

It's when you're in some distant town, on a mission to photograph a rarity of some kind, that the weather gods really seem to tighten their grip. Retford in June 1990 provides just such a case: it's not a town I know at all, so I commit the double crime of taking dull-weather pictures *in the bus station*. But the reward is there in the form of a veteran Leyland Panther of Retford & District — a short-lived initiative of Chesterfield Transport (remember them?).

Above: Even in fog, there's atmosphere in this close-up of a Marshall-bodied Dart of Brighton & Hove, seen on Brighton seafront in May 1997.

Below left: Drab weather, intriguing vehicle: a Northern Counties-bodied Leyland Panther of Retford & District, part of Chesterfield Transport, at Retford bus station in June 1990.

Or take another case: Hartlepool in October 1995. I'm determined to photograph those famous Bristol REs, late survivors of their kind, before their imminent withdrawal. But what does the weather offer? Unremitting drabness. It doesn't flatter the environment, although a newly-pedestrianised area does lift appearances a bit, and some Stagecoach single-deckers look surprisingly cheerful. But the poor old REs, dowdy enough already, look that bit older and sadder in weather like this. Strange to think that it's not just the REs that have disappeared since then; the municipal undertaking itself has gone too.

Dull weather may be a curse, but sunshine can be a fickle friend. If it's late in the year or late in the day, you can get horrendously long shadows and vehicles half-in and half-out of the sun.

It's Aberdeen in August 1986, and I've arrived here late in the day. I charge frantically up and down Union Street, trying to find a decent angle where the buses are sharp but the background isn't blotched out. I gravitate to the bus station, still populated by deep yellow and cream buses of Alexander Northern. I know there must be one spot, somewhere along this short road, where a photograph will work. I finally get a shot of an

Right: **Smart entry treatment (the street, not the bus): a Northern Counties-bodied Dennis Falcon of Stagecoach in Hartlepool in October 1995.**

Left: **On the way out: one of Hartlepool's long-serving Bristol REs, looking notably dowdy on a dull October afternoon in 1995.**

Below: **Evenly lit in the afternoon sun, but it was a close call: an Alexander-bodied Leyland Olympian of Alexander Northern, in Aberdeen in August 1986.**

Alexander-bodied Leyland Olympian, with just about everything evenly lit. Just about.

Jump to Caerphilly in April 1995. Once again, it's late on a sunny day. What I'm actually after is some Dennis Darts in an attractive new maroon Caerphilly Busways livery. Sure enough, I find them up by the railway station, but try as I might, I can't get a shot with the whole bus in the sun. Simply *can't* get one. The one passable view I get there (as it happens) is of an Optare MetroRider of Cardiff City Transport. And the best picture of the day — a rarity, as it turns out — is of a Northern Counties midibus in full Stagecoach livery, trundling down the main street. Ah well, best not to look a gift-horse in the mouth.

If I say Swindon, will you say lamp posts? If you've tried photographing buses there, I think you will. Every time I go there, I find myself irresistibly drawn to Fleming Way, that curving dual carriageway where the buses congregate. And before I know it I'm crouching, squatting, leaning over railings, desperately trying to get a shot that includes buses but not intrusive street furniture.

Once again, digital photography is solving the problem nowadays. If we don't like the lamp posts, the remedy is simple — we just clone them out. I'm not such a purist that I'd condemn this happy solution, although I do sometimes worry that it's making us more sloppy.

In any case, there *are* spots in Swindon where lamp posts aren't a problem. Truly, I've found them. But I have this aversion to taking all my photos from the same position; it seems like copping out, somehow. So having found my ideal location, I usually proceed to abandon it for poorer ones, desperately searching for a second holy grail. Fool to myself?

With all this grief, you might wonder if it's worth bothering. But then there are those occasions when 10 minutes is all you need. In June 1991 I find myself in the Wells area with a little time to spare. It's an opportunity to catch some of Badgerline's

Above: **No lamp posts as this Northern Counties-bodied Dennis Dominator turns into Fleming Way, Swindon, in May 1991.**

Below: **Semi-preserved, a flat-fronted Bristol RE with traditional Bristol scroll fleetname in June 1991. But where is the sun?**

Above: **Bus and cathedral in happy juxtaposition as this rare Alexander-bodied Leyland B21 of Lincoln City Transport surmounts a rise in August 1997.**

very last Bristol REs (a recurring theme, it seems). I don't know the area at all but make my way to the cathedral (not exactly difficult to find), park the car, grab my camera and leap out. And within minutes along comes an RE — right on cue. Not only that, but presently another appears too — this time a venerable flat-fronted model, repainted in traditional Bristol livery.

I can't get the cathedral in the picture, though. That would take preparation, and I don't have the time. Indeed, in Lincoln — another place distinguished by a cathedral — it took me three or four visits over many years before I finally found that one magic stretch of road that's free of pedestrians and turning traffic, where you can get the bus in the foreground and the cathedral on the hill behind it. Don't say I won't keep on trying.

Some shots come more easily. In the summer of 2002 I'm driving out of Seaford, just east of Newhaven, when I spot coming towards me an East Lancs-bodied Dennis double-decker a very

attractive cream-and-maroon version of Brighton & Hove livery. I pull over, casually take out my camera, hold it poised and take the shot. All over in about one minute flat.

If you asked me to nominate a place where I've always found bus photography particularly easy, I'd think I'd say Bournemouth. The hilly town centre is incredibly photogenic, and despite the tourists there seem to be numerous spots where you can get unobstructed views of the traffic. And palm trees.

Strange things have happened to me when I've been taking bus photographs with limited time, but none equals my experience in Derby. I'm hovering outside a civic building of some kind (a police station, I discover), when a policeman unexpectedly accosts me. "What are you doing?" he demands.

Completely wrong-footed, I stare at him wildly. What *am* I doing? Is it illegal? Have I trespassed on some dearly held local by-law or tradition?

"Nothing," I blurt out guiltily. "I was just …"
Just what?

"Then you won't mind giving us ten minutes of your time."

Ten minutes? That's all the time I have left. But I'm so nonplussed that before I know it I'm following

Above: **Approaching Seaford in the summer of 2002, an East Lancs-bodied Dennis Trident of Brighton & Hove, complete with matching flowers.**

Below: **Easy target: an East Lancs-bodied Dennis Lance of Bournemouth's Yellow Buses fleet in September 1997.**

Above: **An East Lancs-bodied Dennis Dart in Derby's smart but short-lived City Rider livery. But an identity parade was shortly to offer an alternative plan.**

him into the building. And here it gradually dawns on me that he wants me to make up the numbers in an identity parade.

"But I'm not from Derby," I tell him weakly.

"Doesn't matter, you don't have to speak. And we'll pay you."

To cut a long story short, I don't have to go on parade after all (some technicality), and they still insist on paying me. I ask to donate the money to some police charity, but they say it's too complicated. They practically force it into my hand and thrust me back on the street — where it's now too late to take any more pictures. Besides, I'd look slightly conspicuous. Feeling somehow robbed in spite of the unwanted beneficence, I skulk away.

Land's End and John O'Groats — two places I've only visited once in my life; so on both occasions I'm eager to celebrate the buses there. I get to Thurso by an epic train journey. (This is the summer of 1986, and they're still running locomotive-hauled trains from Inverness.) I stroll out of the diminutive grey stone station, and there waiting poised for my camera is a Volvo Ailsa of Highland Omnibus, bound for Scrabster Pier. Perfect.

Later I reach John O'Groats on an ageing ECW-bodied Fleetline, which will lay over for just 10 minutes before heading back. With a small bunch of fellow-passengers I stand in the sun, gazing in awe past squat white houses into a brilliant blue seascape. "This is a place to come back to," one of the passengers says quietly. I nod my assent, but I'm torn; I want to prize the moment, but I also need to photograph the Fleetline. I take the shot and return briefly to the contemplation of greater things.

Land's End in September 1991 has less to offer in transport terms, but there's plenty of bus activity in Penzance, the nearest sizeable town. However, I've come here with the new partner in my life, and I'm slightly wary of over-stretching her patience or revealing a side to my character that she might find disconcerting.

"I'm just going to photograph a few buses," I tell her diffidently. She smiles and leans on a railing, watching. "You go ahead." So I snatch a few pictures

Right: **Thurso in August 1986, and an unplanned but effective bit of back-lighting adds interest to this Volvo Ailsa of Highland Scottish.**

Below: **Ten more minutes? Time for this long shot of an ECW-bodied Bristol VRT in Penzance in September 1991.**

of Bristol VRs, Mercedes midis and other miscellaneous vehicles that happen past.

"How are you doing?" I call to her after a while.

"Ten more minutes?" She says it fondly; it's hardly even a question really, and certainly not a request. Yet somehow I feel I must take it as partly both.

I've often found myself reflecting on that comment in the years since then. Who really sets the 10-minute deadline (and I use the term loosely)? Often the timing is dictated by the circumstances, but there's also a self-imposed restraint. Photographing buses may be a kind of madness, but most of the time it stops short of obsession. Keeping a sense of balance is perhaps the greatest trick of all.

WHEN **WAS** THE GOLDEN AGE OF THE BUS?

Depending on how you define the term, it's possible to identify a whole series of Golden Ages for Britain's buses. *David Thrower* explores the possibilities.

In trying to choose a particular Golden Age of the Bus, it is difficult to define exactly when the age of the bus began in the first place. If we take 'bus' to mean motor buses rather than to include horse buses, then we might go back precisely 100 years and opt for 1905 as a starting date, this being when the important operator London Road Car Co purchased eight Clarkson steam buses.

In further support of 1905 as our starting-date, Leyland (trading as the Lancashire Steam Motor Co) exhibited a 30hp Leyland-Crossley in London at the Royal Agricultural Hall. Maudslay, too, exhibited a 40hp bus at the Olympia show in the same year, and the first Straker-Squire 24hp buses went into service with the London Road Car Co. Wolseley too introduced its new range of bus models.

By the end of 1906 there were nearly 800 motor buses working in London. And a year later, the famous if still-primitive Leyland X-type arrived on the scene. The age of the motor bus was truly underway, with total numbers across the UK eventually reaching almost 82,000 by 1965, 10% of them in London. So in 2005 we are looking at roundly a century of motorbus operation — half of it with Routemasters.

Few people reach their own personal century, so there will be virtually no enthusiast who will have first-hand experience of all 10 decades of motor-bus operation. But there will certainly be a few who can look across the span of their lives and recall everything from the later years of the solid-tyred omnibus to today's low-floor, low-emission bendibuses.

Younger enthusiasts will have a much sharper focus, perhaps upon only the last 20 years, or even just the last 10. Many will not even remember conductors outside Central London. So nominating a particular Golden Age really is going to be a matter of personal choice.

And, in any case, how do you judge what to take account of when selecting your choice? Do you opt for the misty-eyed romance of those late-primary-school or early-teenage years, when you were allowed to roam around on your local networks, exploring the world for the first time, Ian Allan *ABC* and rapidly-softening Mars bar in pocket, and with maybe a sneak visit into a bus garage if you were lucky?

Or do you take a hard-nosed business-led view? After all, buses are for carrying people, hence 'omnibus' — 'for all'. An objective view might therefore simply be to look at the operators' annual reports and choose those years when their passenger figures were at their peak and their fleet was at its largest, garages brimming, or even to choose the years when the operation made the greatest profit margin — almost certainly not the same era.

Or should you take pity upon the drivers and (where appropriate) the conductors and remember the era with the best working conditions? After all, it could hardly have been a Golden Age for the driver when he (and it was always 'he' in those days) had to sit unprotected, without even a cab, let alone a cab-heater, beaten by wind and rain. There was nothing romantic about being freezing cold, or peering forward in fog or in gas-lit streets. And there was nothing very 'Golden Age' about crash gears, either. The conductor also wasn't too comfortable on an open-platform bus (usually without heaters) in winter.

So let's allow ourselves a number of Golden Ages...

Private Enterprise

It was a very long while ago, but there once was a time when you could set up a bus company almost at will. In the 1920s there were effectively no town-planning laws, and to start running a service with a couple of buses from, say, a rural motor-repair garage or similar premises was a fairly straightforward matter.

Only in London and other major cities were there any really onerous restrictions. The Metropolitan Police required that a bus should have a maximum wheelbase of 14ft 6in and within a total length of 23ft, the width being no more than 7ft 2in, and should seat a maximum of 18 upstairs and 18 down. There were also severe weight restrictions, and buses were not even allowed to have an enclosed cab or a roof.

By and large, however, the 1920s was the age of the entrepreneur. You have only to take at random a rural area — say, northwest Devon — to see how many operators started at about this time. Ashton of Bideford (1925), Bideford Motor Works (1921), Ensign of Appledore (the early 1920s), Hamlyn, also of Appledore (1920), Ley of Bideford (1923), Oke of Bradworthy (1922), Penwarden of Hartland (1928), Squire of Barnstaple (1919) — it is fascinating to note how so many operators began business in such a short space of time, and this was quite typical of the UK as a whole. Some of these had started as agricultural engineers, others as jobmasters, carriers or hirers of wagonettes; some were former soldiers. Their efforts as small businesses were all too often short-lived, either failing to make enough money or, more usually, being taken over by larger rivals. Amalgamations eventually meant that such areas were soon to be dominated by large well-known operators such as Western National or Devon General.

A few small operators serving niche markets — and a considerable number of coach operators — retained their independence for most of the remainder of the century, or even beyond. But, by and large, it was a case of bigger fish eating little fish, in a way that was to be repeated in the late 1980s. So the early 1920s must qualify as the Golden Age of the Small Operator.

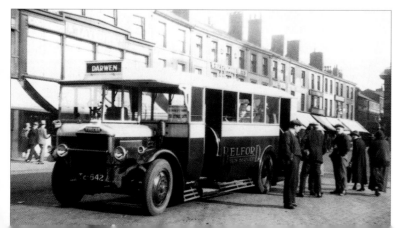

Above: **Among the many small companies to appear in the era after World War 1 was Heysham & District Motors, owner of this 1924 Karrier. The business was acquired by Morecambe & Heysham Corporation in 1929.** *C. Carter*

Left: **Belford Bus Service was a relatively short-lived operation serving Blackburn and Darwen. Its fleet included this Vulcan.** *C. Carter*

Municipal Pride

For Britain's towns and cities, their own Golden Age of bus or trolleybus operation was arguably to start a decade later. There was a protracted era, which could be termed the Golden Age of Municipal Enterprise, stretching from the 1930s through to the end of the 1950s, throughout which there were just under 100 municipal transport operations in the UK.

The 1930s-1950s era of municipal enterprise fell broadly into three periods — the expansionist years of the 1930s, with bus and trolleybus services rapidly extending into the new suburbs, the 1940s, with their rigours of wartime being followed by chronic peacetime shortages, and the 1950s, with fine modern fleets of Leylands, AECs, Daimlers, Guys and Crossleys. By the mid-1950s most municipalities had dispensed with their last trams, and orders for new trolleybuses had slumped to a few dozen per year, so the motor bus — modern, well-maintained and heavily used — really was king of the road in most towns and cities.

Many municipalities and companies were run as a tight ship. A typical example of a well-run municipality was Salford City Transport during the late 1940s and the 1950s, when seemingly the entire fleet would have its roofs, mudguards and wheels given a fresh coat of paint after the end of each winter's weather. And advertising on side panels was banned. After all, this was where the Corporation's crest was to be proudly displayed. Advertising indeed!

By not changing liveries willy-nilly (Sheffield did this in 1952 and very soon regretted it) and by placing repeat orders for standard buses, many operators achieved a quality 'feel', creating a sense of continuity and stability. Southampton, for instance, started ordering Guy Arabs in 1934 and by the late 1940s was addicted to the type, going back for more and more until most of the fleet comprised plum-and-off-white Arabs with silver roofs. The operator always seemed to turn out clean buses with fresh paintwork, although at the end of the war its tramcars, like those of many other fleets, had looked spectacularly decrepit.

Another quality operator — and one that seemed to exist in an almost-permanent Golden Age from the start of the 1930s till the end of the 1960s — was Birmingham City Transport, whose blue-and-cream buses always exuded civic pride and

Below: **The highest of municipal standards were maintained by Edinburgh Corporation, whose mainly Leyland fleet also featured a number of Guys, including this Alexander-bodied Arab IV.** *Stewart J. Brown*

Above right: **Leeds could be counted among the biggest of Britain's municipal bus fleets, operating in a distinctive if somewhat sombre two-tone green. This Daimler CVG6-30 had bodywork built by local builder Charles H. Roe. Note the conductor with his Ultimate ticket machine.** *Alan D. Broughall*

evidence of the highest standards of care and maintenance. Nottingham too always looked good, though its livery couldn't match Brum's.

North of the border there were many fine fleets during the 1930s and 1950s, none seemingly better cared for than Edinburgh's. The city is often cited for the infamous quote that its Orion buses were 'monstrous masses of shivering tin', but it should really be best remembered for its splendid madder-and-white livery, seemingly always shining amidst the grey stonework of the capital's fine architecture. Was there ever such a thing as a scruffy Edinburgh bus? One strongly doubts it.

The other cities of Scotland were no less proud, and high standards of public transport were an integral part of municipal pride, giving a sense not just of community ownership but of civic integration, marking out each city much as today's seem to be dominated (at least, as far as their fans are concerned) by the colours of football shirts. This applied even more so in those parts of England where towns and cities became near-contiguous. The identities of such places as St Helens, Wigan, Bolton, Bury and Rochdale couldn't possibly be confused with each other, nor could places such as Todmorden, Halifax, Huddersfield and Bradford. Each was utterly unmistakable.

The Golden Age of the Municipal Trolleybus was, in retrospect, surprisingly brief, many fleets purchasing large numbers of fine new vehicles in the late 1930s only to see preference being given to bus expansion by the late 1950s. In 1939 the 34 trolleybus systems outside London — most of them municipally owned — mustered a combined fleet of 1,831 trolleybuses. In 1953 the 33 systems then operational (again, excluding London) were running 2,552 vehicles, so there was still expansion. Yet by the mid-1960s closures were raining down on the beleaguered trolleybus, and by 1972 it was all over. There was a Golden Age of the Trolleybus, but it was barely two decades long, and one of those was scarred by war.

Rear Engines

Perhaps there are two types of bus aficionado — those who were born BA (Before Atlantean) and those born AA. Nearly 50 years after it first appeared the rear-engined bus still causes furrowed brows, many maintaining that the half-cab era was the only true Golden Age.

But it is very easy to argue that moving the engine to the back and installing doors at the front, whilst still keeping the conductor, was in some ways the very best of all worlds. So was there a Golden Age of the Atlantean and Fleetline, perhaps even including the VR as well?

Certainly there were cities that really went rear-engined in a big way. Liverpool placed into service several large batches of Atlanteans, Nos L500-699 arriving in the period 1962-4, L700-759 in 1965/6 and L760-879 in 1966/7, so that, by the time it was subsumed into the Merseyside Passenger Transport Executive, it had a fleet of nearly 400 modern rear-engined buses — a notable and praiseworthy achievement.

Newcastle also went for the Atlantean, with almost 160 by 1965, rising to 210 by 1967. Glasgow, of course, took one of the very first Atlanteans and had 200 by the end of 1963. Other municipalities were slower off the mark; Bradford, for example, initially eschewed the rear-engined bus but after 1967 bought batches of both the Atlantean and the rival Fleetline.

The PTE era could be argued to have been a second, Golden Age of the Atlantean, in its descendant AN68 version, and of the evergreen Fleetline. SELNEC/Greater Manchester, for example, inherited large numbers of PDR1 Atlanteans or Fleetlines from Manchester, Salford, Bolton, Bury, Rochdale, Oldham, Ashton-under-Lyne, SHMD and, at a later date Wigan and Lancashire United. It then went on to order its own AN68s, buying large batches of 'Standards' (as they were termed) between 1972 and 1984, numbered almost consecutively from 7001 to 8765. Other PTEs did likewise.

The late 1970s could certainly be regarded as the Golden Age for Greater Manchester PTE in terms of standardisation, though other elements of a Golden Age, such as reliability, efficiency and courtesy were less certain. And the earlier, pre-PTE benefits of having conductors gradually faded away, until the last went in 1986.

Left: **Early rear-engined double-deckers were uncompromisingly square, but Alexander brought new style to the breed with this body. Developed originally for Glasgow Corporation, it soon found favour elsewhere, including Newcastle, owner of this 1966 bus with panoramic windows.** *Alan D. Broughall*

Below: **Pioneering work by SELNEC PTE created a new and neat 'Standard' design for rear-engined double-deckers. Bodies to this design were built by both Northern Counties and Park Royal on Fleetline and Atlantean chassis. A Fleetline loads in Warrington bus station in 1982.** *Stewart J. Brown*

The Giants

Outside the cities and large towns much of the bus network of the 1950s and 1960s was dominated by the Tilling and BET groups, including giants such as BET-owned Midland Red. Tilling and BET created something of a patchwork quilt, filling in large tracts of countryside between major urban areas, such as across South Tyneside and County Durham, and with heavy penetrating flows into the adjacent municipal areas. Some urban centres were themselves predominantly Tilling, such as Bristol Omnibus, or BET, such as Gateshead & District.

The Tilling Group had a highly standardised range of vehicles, and this produced its own Golden Age, that of the K and L types, later supplemented by the Lodekka and the MW, to be followed by the VR and the RE. And Tilling was popular, at least with enthusiasts. In a magazine reader poll, seeking nominations for future diecast model prototypes, the humble Bristol Lodekka came out top.

fleet carried an incredible 385 million passengers, and a decade later this had fallen by only 11%, to 341 million. Its motorway services to London were amongst the best-known in the industry.

Further north, Ribble was another giant, although it didn't knit its own buses the way that Midland Red did. From a fleet of under a hundred in the early 1920s it grew to nearly 1,200 by the 1950s and still stood at 800 in the early 1980s. And, again, its express services were famous.

There were also many southern companies that stood out in the crowd, particularly Maidstone & District, East Kent, Southdown and Aldershot & District. From a fleet of 30 buses in 1914, A&D had grown to a fleet of approaching 400 by 1950. Its image was second to none. When it was swallowed up into Alder Valley, the result was not an improvement. Each of these companies enjoyed lengthy Golden Ages that seemed to last until the 1960s but no further.

Left: **Most of those urban areas in England and Wales which were not served by a municipal bus fleet were catered for by BET. In the North East of England there were municipal fleets, but inter-urban services and routes in many of the smaller towns in County Durham were provided by BET subsidiary Northern General. Two Routemasters are seen when new.** *Geoff Coxon*

Below: **Maidstone & District was a well-respected BET business serving much of Kent. This is a Bristol K, unusual in having been rebodied with a Metro-Cammell Orion body.** *Stewart J. Brown*

There was something very familiar, almost slightly dull, about the Tilling empire in the late 1950s and early 1960s, with the K/L/MW and later the Lodekka/RE/VR types all looking very much part of the same family, be it Western National or Eastern Scottish, or more geographically incognito fleets such as United Counties.

A different beast altogether was Midland Red, building its own idiosyncratic buses and operating across a vast swathe of Middle England, from Banbury to Birmingham, from Leamington to Leicester and from Shrewsbury to Stafford. In many ways it was an extraordinary, larger-than-life company. In 1954 its 1,900-strong bus and coach

Right: **With a fleet of around 2,000 vehicles Midland Red was for many years Britain's biggest bus operator after London Transport. It built its own buses, including the distinctive integral D9 double-decker. This one is seen in Leicester in 1973, after Midland Red had become part of NBC.**
Stewart J. Brown

Left: **Tilling Group companies served large parts of England and Wales until the formation of the National Bus Company in 1969. Typifying the Tilling fleet is this 1966 Bristol Omnibus FLF Lodekka in Swindon.**
Stewart J. Brown

Below: **Ribble had been one of BET's biggest subsidiaries and remained a giant within NBC. Most of its buses were built by Leyland, including this National 2 in Blackburn bus station in 1982.**
Stewart J. Brown

Right: **Well-proportioned bodywork by Massey of Wigan is complemented by AEC's handsome bonnet and grille on this Colchester Corporation Regent V. New in 1956, it was photographed in 1973.**
Stewart J. Brown

Travelling in Style

Was there ever a Golden Age of Bus Design? Good design has always been a part of bus travel, sometimes very good indeed, at other times less so.

Bus interiors have moved from the polished woodwork and painted or rexine surfaces of the 1940s to the 'hairy carpet' walls and plastic coatings of the present day, having in some areas passed through an unhappy interim phase of vinyl seats, as on some 1970s models, such as the Leyland National. There could therefore be argued to have been two Golden Ages for interiors, one in the 1930s and the other today. Modern buses are well-lit, well-heated and hard-wearing. And cloth seat covers still offer attractive patterns and styles. In many ways, things have never been better, particularly in terms of accessibility.

But it is the overall design of the bus's or trolleybus's exterior, rather than interior, that probably lies at the very heart of most enthusiasts' interest in bus transport as a hobby. The divided radiator of the AEC, the rear upper-deck of the 1940s Leyland Farington body, the bonnet of the immortal Routemaster, the somehow benign 'smiling face' of the front of a 1930s trolleybus, the roof of a 'Beverley Bar' bus … all are individual design classics. Only rarely did the industry produce an ugly bus or coach — the Daimler CD650, with its enormous snout, and the Crellin-Duplex coaching monstrosity of the 1950s come to mind — although we are really looking at buses here, rather than coaches, the latter being a topic in itself.

Was there a Golden Age of Publicity? Few operators outside London produced good publicity prior to the PTE era. Apart from small timetables and the occasional map, for most municipalities and other operators that was about it. However, the new

PTE organisations really did try hard in this area, with clearer timetables, easy-to-read bus maps and other special promotional material to encourage bus travel. Unfortunately, some of the effect was lost at deregulation, but, by and large, the PTEs persevered and thus do deserve a Golden Age award for their efforts.

And when was the Golden Age of Liveries? The external colour of buses has always aroused disproportionate passion — after all, if it's on time, you get a seat, the driver doesn't insult you and the fare is cheap, does the colour matter that much to the ordinary passenger? But to the enthusiast, and to those who consider the streetscape to be part of the wider quality of life, a bus in a tasteful livery can considerably enhance the urban scene. London's red double-deckers are reputedly one of the most important features of the city that are quoted by tourists, so the colour (at least in the Central Zone) has become a fixture.

But other famous liveries, such as Glasgow's green and orange, Newcastle's striking yellow, Bradford's blue, Manchester's vermilion and Birmingham's blue and cream, have all vanished, and we are all much the poorer for that. Outside the major cities, liveries such as Southdown's, East Yorkshire's, Alexander's blue or maroon, all these too have gone.

And although we still have a few traditional liveries around, and some of the new ones are passably good, there is definitely a feeling that we are now in the visual doldrums, with vinyl stripes and sometimes garish colours. And you cannot beam yourself down onto the streets of a city or town nowadays and know at once where you are, in the way you usually could before 1986.

So the Golden Age of Liveries might well be any

time from, say, the 1920s to the early 1980s — most of the century, in fact. Perhaps one day the swoops-and-stripes liveries on white-based backgrounds will finally disappear. After all, it costs no more to adopt a pleasing livery than a visually discordant one.

Incidentally, swoops haven't always been a bad thing. Manchester Corporation, Rochdale, Kingston-upon-Hull and one or two other operators have, at times, dared to be different and have succeeded in creating stylish liveries that actually worked well. More recently, in the late 1980s, the second-life North Western Road Car had an interesting part-blue, part-red livery, the divide running diagonally from the front corner of the roofline, and it looked surprisingly good, though it was abandoned in the early 1990s.

Deregulation

And that brings us to deregulation. The 1985 Transport Act, more notoriously known to the public as bus deregulation, was meant to usher in a new golden age, in which the customer was king, the staff were more motivated (and, where possible, owned their own buses), and where costs were cut to the point where much of the mileage that had been lost since the 1950s could be viable once again.

Bus deregulation would, of course, fill a book in itself. There was much that was good about it, and much that was bad. Some of the good things didn't last, and some of the bad things resulted from its botched implementation.

The year 1986 put hundreds of extra buses onto the streets of those cities where competition was hottest — notably Glasgow and in Manchester, where huge 'bus jams' made the headlines. Many of these extra buses were elderly specimens from elsewhere, some of Glasgow's being ex-London Routemasters, and some of Manchester's including third-hand (via Western National) former London DMSs, as well as other even more exotic third-hand specimens, such as Leyland Panthers dragged back from the Isle of Man. Sales of new buses slumped as operators tried to compete on cost rather than quality.

The architects of bus deregulation had dreamed of creating a climate where new operators sprang up, starting new services and charging keen fares. But in truth it wasn't that sort of world any more. There might not have been such strict control of route licensing, but the post-1986 world bristled with more regulations, of other sorts, than ever. Planning laws, employment laws, Health & Safety, Ministry vehicle checks, competition laws … the list was endless. Operators couldn't even agree among themselves to provide balanced headways without consulting the competition authorities — a ludicrous situation.

Much was made at the time of innovative practices, such as new minibuses and more proactive marketing, but these too were more questionable than they at first seemed. Most of the minibuses had vanished by the end of the century, without direct replacement. The Golden Age of the Minibus was brief indeed, lasting from about 1986 to about 1990.

Some (though not all) frequencies were massively improved, only to be cut back once more a couple of years later. And supposedly improved marketing included reprehensible tactics such as showing only your own company's workings in the timetable — even if this meant implying that a route ran evenings and Sundays only — and the non-acceptance of rival operators' tickets. Whilst bus operators played these childish war-games with

Below: **One of the success stories of deregulation was Black Prince of Leeds, which built up a smart fleet, mainly buying second-hand buses. This Marshall-bodied Scania came from Newport Transport.** *Stewart J. Brown*

each other, car ownership and use soared.

For many (though not all) passengers, deregulation was thus the Lost Age, rather than the Golden Age, and in terms of vehicle quality it was often a Dark Age. Only in the late 1990s did stability return, with the purchase of new buses, the scrapping of most of the superannuated specimens and the realisation that a total free-for-all was not the universal solution.

But in an unorthodox and ironic way, the 1986-96 period was, if only for the detached observer, a curious sort of Golden Age — an age of turmoil, uncertainty, new operators and takeovers, mergers and withdrawals, lost licences and warnings. 'May you live in interesting times' is reputed to be an old Chinese curse, and was there ever a more interesting time? For the passengers (and staff) it was chaos, but there was never a dull moment during those first few years of deregulation, and it is unlikely that we will ever see such a period again.

London

And now we come finally to London. London inevitably dominates any debate about Golden Ages. In a recent poll of readers to ascertain the all-time-classic bus of the 20th century, the magazine *Classic Bus* reported that 48% nominated either the Routemaster or the RT, with separate polls for double- or single-deckers again being dominated by these two designs together with the RF single-decker.

For many enthusiasts aged over 50, the London Transport of the immediate postwar era will therefore be their definitive Golden Age. The London Transport of the time seemed invincible, with an almost mystical status. Despite wartime maintenance backlogs and a run-down fleet of buses, trams and trolleybuses it coped with unprecedented levels of demand, culminating in a near-standardised bus fleet. The bus, tram and trolleybus fleets, driven by 23,000 drivers, operated from a staggering 111 garages and depots.

The scale of this organisation took (and still takes) some absorbing. And the levels of patronage in the early postwar years were stunning. In 1949 London's motor buses and Green Line coaches carried 2.75 billion passengers, the equivalent of about 60 times the entire UK population. This was in addition to 292 million tram journeys and 891 million trolleybus journeys. The grand annual total of nearly four billion journeys was the equivalent of nearly *ninety* times the total UK population — and that wasn't counting the Underground.

And the books still balanced — just. In 1953 LT's road services cost £50 million and revenue also stood at £50 million. This was the last time this would occur, of course, and the capital's transport system was to slither downhill financially for decades to come, caught in a vicious circle of fare increases, traffic congestion and falling patronage, not to mention a fruitless seven-week strike in 1958.

To traditionalists, even the hybrid Routemaster/RT era of the 1960s might also seem like a later Golden Age, with thousands of RMs and RTs, plus 700 RF single-deckers, making up the bulk of the fleet. In the early 1960s vehicle maintenance was still generally good, the fleet was well presented and reliable, and the traditional London Transport of the 1930s, with its emphasis on quality and standardisation, was still clearly discernible.

But behind the scenes, matters were much less happy. Staff shortages were becoming critical, and management practices were wasteful. The arrival of one-man (later 'one-person') -operated buses sent

Above: **Is this the new Golden Age? A Metroline Dennis Trident with Alexander ALX400 body typifies the new breed of low-floor double-deckers which has flooded into the capital in the early years of the 21st century. But Routemasters still abound in Oxford Street in 2004.** *Stewart J. Brown*

the organisation into a mechanical-unreliability nosedive from which it seemed incapable of recovering. Running the service became a nightmare of continuous staff and vehicle-parts shortages. New bus types came and went, sometimes with dizzy speed. Even actually getting rid of unwanted buses became a crisis, with hundreds of redundant AEC Swifts stored on Radlett Aerodrome. The 1950s began to assume an even rosier image by comparison.

And the fleet shrank remorselessly, prompting garage closures. From a total (including trolleybuses) of nearly 9,700 in 1955, which could be viewed as the height of the 'RT era', the number of buses had fallen to 7,900 in 1968 and then dipped to 6,400 after the loss in 1970 of the former Country Area. By 1988 it would sink further, to 5,000 — virtually half the 1955 level, though of course the operating area was smaller.

The early 1980s saw a particularly turbulent period in London's bus fortunes. Under Ken Livingstone's radical Greater London Council the October 1981 'Fares Fair' scheme saw a 32% reduction in fares and a 10% jump in patronage. But the lowest point of all, arguably, was when the notorious Law Lords decision was given in March 1982, upholding Bromley Council's view that fare subsidies were unlawful. Fares were then hiked by an unforgettable 96% and patronage slumped back by 18%. This was followed by a 25% fares cut in May 1983, subsequently accompanied by a 12% rise in passengers.

But much damage had been done. Again, it was the very opposite of a Golden Age. Large numbers of Routemasters were instantly withdrawn and

started to make their way to Barnsley for scrapping — a tragic sight for their devotees. Yet London was later to be spared the deregulation chaos that erupted elsewhere in Britain, a system of tendering a network that was centrally planned and co-ordinated being adopted instead.

Although for a while there was a degree of instability, and the traditional red livery itself seemed threatened, London pulled through. Savings were made in service provision. New initiatives were launched, and new buses ordered. Whilst patronage was falling elsewhere, it began to rise again in the capital. Even some Routemasters were bought back from their latter-day owners and renovated for fresh service on London's streets. The RM era is now drawing to a close, but London is seeing steady passenger growth and an impressive influx of new accessible buses. Congestion Charging has also been unexpectedly successful in reducing the effects of the private car upon bus journey times. And we have bendi-buses, kneeling buses, leaning-leftwards-at-stops buses, low-emission buses … the technology has never been more varied, nor the London public more enthusiastically wooed.

So, to answer the title question, although the remainder of the UK mainland can only look on with envy, for Londoners perhaps *now* is the real Golden Age of the Bus …

UNDER THE

All photographs by the autho

WIRES

Roy Marshall looks at trolleybuses in Britain and reminisces on some of his early encounters with them.

between the late war years and the 1950s I travelled around the UK to visit all the existing trolleybus systems.

During the war I got to know a tower-wagon driver and his two overhead linesmen based at Nottingham Corporation's Trent Bridge depot. Sometimes on a Sunday I would go out with them on line inspection, and I learned a lot from them. During the working day two crews were on duty — one on inspection and one on standby. This did not change until the use of radio telephones meant that the inspection crew could be called to emergencies such as a damaged trolley-head.

Also during the war a change took place with the replacement of trolley-wheels by sliding heads with carbon inserts, to avoid sparking at 'frogs' and crossovers which could have been seen by enemy aircraft in hours of darkness. Not all operators changed; Birmingham and Notts & Derby, for example, did not. The latter found that a carbon insert would not last a full day's work in its high operating area, especially in frosty weather.

With the loss of so many male employees to

the armed forces during the war, females were recruited with some becoming drivers and others conductresses. There are stories of slightly-built women, attempting to transfer the spring-loaded trolley-booms to or from the running wires using the bamboo pole, being hoisted into the air by the strength of the springs.

The growth of road traffic brought changes in traffic control, including the use of roundabouts at road junctions, and I was fascinated by the way new overhead for such junction improvements would be erected overnight over the top of the existing wires and then, on a Saturday/Sunday night, the old wiring cut down and the new lowered into place.

The traffic growth also brought problems, with trolleybus drivers often being forced to brake and come to a halt on a 'dead' section. Usually a gradient would allow the vehicle to coast backwards or forwards onto a live section, but increasingly battery-powered manœuvres became commonplace.

Happy days.

Right: The driver of a prewar Bradford AEC 661T re-connects his bus to the overhead wires in Forster Square in 1948. The long pole he is using was transported in a carrier under the bus. English Electric built the bodywork.

Left: In 1939 Brighton Corporation purchased 44 Weymann-bodied AEC trolleybuses for tram replacement. Note that these carried both the municipal crest and the Brighton Hove & District fleetname, as services were operated jointly between the Corporation and Tilling-owned BH&D.

Below: In 1952 Doncaster Corporation purchased six three-year-old East Lancs-bodied BUT 9611Ts from Darlington, which had decided to abandon trolleybus operation — and, indeed, had tried to sell these BUTs before they were delivered. They would serve Doncaster until 1959, being then sold for further service in Bradford.

Left: Between 1958 and 1962 Bournemouth purchased 19 Sunbeam MF2B models with attractive dual-door Weymann bodies; there should have been 20, but one was destroyed by a fire at the Weymann factory. Had trolleybuses remained popular, vehicles such as this, with an entrance ahead of the front axle, would have been suitable for one-person operation. Note the Austin A40 van on the left and the later A40 Farina on the right. This is a 1964 view.

Left: In 1936 Grimsby Corporation purchased impressive Roe-bodied AEC 664Ts, one of which is seen in neighbouring Cleethorpes in 1948, in the company of a postwar Roe-bodied Karrier. Passengers are exhorted to 'Take Fynnon Salt for Rheumatism'.

Right: A busy scene in Ipswich in 1958, with the last Ransomes trolleybus to enter UK service. Originally built as a demonstrator for South Africa, that plan was foiled by the outbreak of war and it was purchased instead by Ipswich, in 1940. Massey built the stylish body. Other vehicles in the picture include two Morris Minors and an Austin A40 van.

Left: A Karrier W with Park Royal body in the Maidstone fleet, at Barming's Bull Inn terminus. In 1958 the Chatham Reliance Building Society was offering 3% interest — and bank rates were sufficiently stable for this to be advertised on a painted advert on the front of the bus.

Right: Manchester trolleybuses lined up in Piccadilly in 1959. The lead vehicle is a locally-built Crossley TDD64/1, with 66-seat Crossley bodywork, supplied in 1951. Behind is a two-axle 58-seater of 1950, while at the rear are two BUT 9612Ts with Burlingham bodies from a batch of 62 delivered in 1955/6.

Left: Single-deck trolleybuses required long booms, as illustrated by this Mexborough & Swinton Sunbeam W with centre-entrance Brush body, seen at Conisburgh ready to depart for Rotherham. Mexborough & Swinton was a subsidiary of the BET group.

Right: The smart appearance of this 1941 Weymann-bodied AEC in the Notts & Derby fleet in March 1953 belies the fact that the system is about to be closed. When closure came, in April, the entire 31-vehicle fleet was sold to Bradford Corporation and replaced by Bristol KSW and AEC Regent III motor buses.

Right: **Reading** Corporation was an early user of platform doors as a way of reducing accidents involving passengers boarding or alighting. This Sunbeam S7 with 68-seat Park Royal body was new in 1950 and was one of 12 operated until the system's replacement by motor buses in 1968.

Left: Trolleybuses with side-gangway lowbridge bodies were relatively unusual. The only utility examples were for St Helens and included 10 1945 Sunbeam Ws bodied by Roe. Most were withdrawn in 1956. The system closed in 1958.

Right: The roadway under this bridge was lowered to allow double-deck buses to pass through, and the first double-deck trolleybuses in the fleet of the Teesside Railless Traction Board were eight Sunbeam Ws delivered in 1944, one of which is seen here squeezing through on its way to North Ormesby. This bus had a 56-seat Weymann body and was still in use — having been fitted with a new Roe body in 1962 — when TRTB was absorbed by Teesside Municipal Transport in 1968.

Left: Walsall bought 15 three-axle Sunbeam MS2s for the service to Bloxwich. This one, bodied by Weymann, is seen in the town centre in 1949.

Right: The use by one operator of trolleybuses belonging to another was rare. This Glasgow BUT RETB was tried both by Nottingham and, as seen here, by Walsall in 1953 before being delivered to its owner. It had an East Lancs body and was designed for pay-as-you-enter operation, with passengers entering at the rear and paying a seated conductor.

Left: In 1938/9 a fleet of 14 Roe-bodied Daimler CTM4s entered service with West Hartlepool, although six were actually owned by neighbouring Hartlepool. The use of top-sliding vents was unusual at a time when most buses had half-drop windows.

TRAVEL AROUND A
WORLD
HERITAGE SITE

Michael H. C. Baker takes a fond look at transport in the Telford area.

Long ago, when I first knew the Telford area, Wellington was much the most important place thereabouts. Its Midland Red garage supplied nearly all the buses which served the district, while its station was an important junction where expresses from Paddington to Shrewsbury, Birkenhead and the Cambrian coast always called, and where branches to Market Drayton and Crewe, to Buildwas, Much Wenlock and Craven Arms, to Coalport and to Stafford all diverged.

And Telford, as such, did not exist.

My mother came from a rural community some half-dozen miles north of Shrewsbury and, having met and married Dad, moved to South London, but at least once a year we would visit relations there, travelling by GWR (and, later, BR Western Region) express from Paddington. Wellington was the last stop before Shrewsbury, where we would change to an LMS Crewe-bound stopping train, alighting at Hadnall and walking the last two miles, usually with our luggage balanced on the carrier of the bike belonging to mum's older sister, Aunt Agnes, who had met us at the station.

Aunt Agnes's husband, Uncle Frank, was cowman on a large farm belonging to an estate where members of my family had been employed for generations. It was an intensely rural area, and their cottage was one of a group of three, next door being occupied by Mr Paling, a tractor driver whose large family seemed to increase on each visit, and the one beyond by Mr Parry, the farm's lorry driver.

The cottages, although only two fields away from the railway, were a long way from the station and almost as far from the nearest bus stop. This was at Sansaw Turn, just up the road from the cottage where mum had been brought up, by her

Left: **At Midland Red's Shrewsbury garage in 1956 stand a 1934 CON (left) and a 1935 DON. Their narrow cabs gave them a particularly antiquated appearance.** *Michael H. C. Baker*

Above right: **In sharp contrast Midland Red's postwar fleet was ahead of its time, with underfloor-engined single-deckers and double-deckers which had concealed radiators. This line-up was also photographed at Shrewsbury garage in 1956.** *Michael H. C. Baker*

grandmother and Aunt Hatt, her father having been killed at Gallipoli in World War 1 and her mother dying soon after.

Sansaw was not overburdened with buses, but being in the depths of the country did as well as could be expected. It was served by the 990, very nearly the highest-numbered of the vast network of routes operated by Midland Red, which in the 1940s and 1950s covered a larger area of England than any other operator, and by the 986, a route it shared with Salopia Saloon Coaches. There were two buses a day Monday to Fridays, an extra two on Wednesdays, an extra one on Thursdays, four on Saturdays and none on Sundays, all going to Shrewsbury, 27 minutes away.

Truth to tell, we mostly used the train when going to Shrewsbury, or, in the other direction, to Wem on market day, or further east to Whitchurch, whence came Uncle Frank's family. However, we did take the bus to Shrewsbury, or attempted to. I can remember one occasion as a very small boy, around 1942, standing at Sansaw Turn waiting for the mid-day bus only for it to draw up, and the conductor to lean out and inform us that his vehicle was full to overflowing, with not even standing room; then, with a 'ding-ding', off he went, leaving us and several others with no alternative but to trudge the mile and a half home and give up all thoughts of an afternoon at the pictures at the Granada, Castle Hill, with tea afterwards.

I was deeply disappointed, for Midland Red buses were like none I had ever seen before. Officially their silver roofs were painted over during the war, but I'm sure some serving rural areas escaped, for this feature was my first impression of them. My second was how extraordinarily old-fashioned they looked, with their narrow cabs, high bodies, minimal wings and wooden indicator boards. Single-deckers

were rare beasts in my part of Surrey, but those I had come across were either Qs, which were about as up-to-date as you could get, or six-wheeled LTs, which, although no younger than the average Midland Red bus, certainly didn't look half as archaic.

Expeditions from my aunt's to picturesque Ellesmere, known locally as The Lake District of Shropshire, were more successful. This involved another long walk, which no-one in the country in those days thought twice about — a good two miles to Harmer Hill, where the rather more frequent 981 plied its trade. This journey took 34 minutes and deposited us at the most northwesterly extremity of the Midland Red empire and virtually within a Welsh male-voice choir of the border.

Ellesmere was one of the many frontier posts with Crosville; Oswestry was another. Although a Tilling company, in the late 1940s and early 1950s

Below: **On services from Chester to Gobowen in the mid-1950s Crosville would often use a prewar Leyland Titan, such as this 1938 TD5 with six-bay lowbridge ECW body, photographed in Chester in 1955 with a Bristol L behind.** *Michael H. C. Baker*

Above: **A Mid Wales Motorways Sentinel in Shrewsbury in 1955 on the service to Newtown. Note the driver's door — an unusual feature on an underfloor-engined bus.** *Michael H. C. Baker*

Crosville still possessed a fascinating variety of non-Bristols, often Leylands, quite often with non-ECW bodies. In the mid-1960s I used to travel from Chester to visit Great Aunt Hatt, by then living at Gobowen, near Oswestry, and almost always found myself in a Lodekka, usually a rear-entrance FS, although once a K-type (by then an endangered species) was provided, but 10 years earlier Chester garage might have put out prewar Titans, some more than 20 years old.

There were also a great many small independents working (as there still are) all along the Marches, from the Wirral right down to the Severn Estuary; I even came across an ex-London Transport STL in Oswestry, around 1954. Vaggs of Knockin Heath and Salopia operated northwest of Shrewsbury and up towards the border, although I don't think the STL belonged to either of these. Double-deckers were very much the exception, there being little call, except on school runs, for such large vehicles; nor, indeed, would they have negotiated many of the lanes in the sparsely populated, hilly countryside where the independents operated on both the English and Welsh sides of the border.

Shrewsbury garage worked all Midland Red services in north Shropshire. It is still there, on what was the A49 before successive by-passes were built, in the northeast suburbs and close to the Sentinel works, another survivor from long ago. Although the garage is now painted in Arriva colours, the legend 'Midland Red' is still there for all to see, in bold letters over the entrance. Sentinel, like Midland Red, was a pioneer of underfloor-engined buses in the late 1940s and early 1950s, beating the giants — Leyland, AEC and others — into production. Although it never rivalled them in numbers it sold well in the Midlands, and Mid Wales Motorways used several Beadle-bodied examples on its route from Newtown, in Montgomeryshire, into Shrewsbury. Some 10 journeys were operated weekdays, and although Newtown was shown on the indicator passengers actually changed at Welshpool. The two-hour overall journey time was in direct competition with the railways: a stopping train took around 1hr 40min, the 'Cambrian Coast Express', stopping only at Welshpool and Montgomery, an hour and a quarter.

South of Shrewsbury, being mostly bereft of relations, was virtually unknown territory. As I grew older and began to take more interest in the history of Shropshire I realised that the area around Ironbridge, Wellington and Coalport was very different from rural north Shropshire, being nothing less than the birthplace of the Industrial Revolution. So one day in May 1956 I decided it was time to explore.

In those days, the best part of 50 years ago, there was still a feeling that things Victorian were old-fashioned but not so remote as to be historically interesting — my grandmother, born in 1861, was still alive — so they were still being discarded without much thought. The iron bridge itself, being the first in the world built of iron and clearly unique (and pre-Victorian) was considered of some interest, although clearly not in the same league as, say, Stonehenge or the site of the medieval Battle of Shrewsbury — even though there's nothing to see of that except pleasant green fields. But hardly anybody paid any heed to the overgrown, decaying, practically vanished remnants dotted all around the district of Coalbrookdale. Yet this was where the Industrial Revolution — and thus the modern world — began. Now, of course, it is a World Heritage Site.

In 1956 there were five scheduled trips from Shrewsbury to Ironbridge, all but one continuing on up the hill to Madeley. Four of them were on route X93, which took 40 minutes. The fifth was the 975, which, not being an express service, dawdled its way through Atcham, Easton Constantine Turn, Leighton and Buildwas — and took a whole three minutes longer! But this was not unusual within the Midland Red empire, wherein a large number of 'X' services were operated, often covering quite long distances but stopping more or less where required.

Left: **A rebuilt SON with top-sliding windows climbs Dawley Bank on its way to Ironbridge in 1956. The bus was new in 1936.**
Michael H. C. Baker

Right: **A later (1940) SON climbs one of the steep hills out of Ironbridge in 1956.**
Michael H. C. Baker

As in so many other parts of Shropshire in the steam era, there were competing train services. In this instance the result was a draw, the five trains taking between 39 and 42 minutes. They continued on to Bridgnorth, and several went further south to

Above: **Midland Red's Wellington garage in 1956, with a rebuilt 1939 SON.** *Michael H. C. Baker*

Below: **Midland Red contrast. It's hard to believe that only two years separate these vehicles. The SON bus on the left was built in 1937, while the ONC coach on the right dated from 1939. By the standards of the late 1930s the SON was old-fashioned, while the ONC was the ultimate in modernity.** *Michael H. C. Baker*

Bewdley, along what is now the Severn Valley Railway. I did have some south Shropshire relations, in Bridgnorth, and they always favoured Midland Red's 964 on journeys to and from Shrewsbury, rather than the train; again, the overall journey time was almost the same, but they said they found the bus more convenient. Certainly the 964 was more frequent, with nine journeys in each direction on weekdays. The bus took a different route from the train, via Much Wenlock instead of Ironbridge. The former is a remarkably pretty town and in the 1950s was probably more famous than Ironbridge, having been the setting for a feature film. I was told this by a young lady who lived in Bridgnorth and on whom I developed a severe crush. You'd have thought I would have hung on her every word; perhaps I did, but 50 years later the film's name — though not hers — quite escapes me.

Having admired the bridge, which was certainly not overburdened with sightseers, I headed for Wellington. A complex series of routes linked Ironbridge and Wellington by way of Coalbrookdale, Madeley, Little Dawley, Dawley, Lawley and Horsehay, the journey time varying between 28 and 36 minutes.

Wellington garage was home to a large and varied collection of Midland Red single-deck buses and coaches. Despite the antique looks of prewar Midland Red single-deckers they were built to last, and did. A good many were rebuilt immediately after World War 2, but even some of those in original condition lasted 20 years. Rebuilt examples were readily identifiable by their slide-vent windows and lack of mouldings. Although in original condition it may have looked old-fashioned, the standard prewar Midland Red single-decker, the SON, simply oozed personality and character, and in most cases the rebuilding did nothing to destroy this. No fewer than 330 SONs were built, a few being sold to Trent. The final two batches, the FHAs and GHAs (the HA registration, Smethwick, was one of the most characteristic features of Midland Red vehicles), had modernised radiators, whilst the GHAs had a new, smoother body style and all-red roofs — but were still rather nice. Wellington garage operated examples of all these, although by 1956 many of the earlier SONs had been withdrawn, whilst others were having their distinctive silver roofs painted red.

Coaches for private-hire and excursion work also lived at Wellington, and I came across some of the final prewar ONCs at home there. Midland Red was quite incapable of producing a vehicle which lacked distinction and originality, and the ONCs with their full fronts and sweeping lines had more than a hint of art deco and streamlining. By this date they had given up regular express services except at summer weekends, when many buses would also be pressed into service on lengthy journeys to London, Blackpool, Rhyl and East Coast resorts — an experience I don't regret missing out on.

In October 2003 I stayed with wife and friends in a cottage overlooking Ironbridge Gorge. The cottage at the end of the street sported a neat, blue, round plaque proclaiming that Billy Wright was born there. Billy Wright was one of the greatest English footballers of the immediate postwar era, captain both of Wolves, when they were England's top team and pioneers of European football, and of England. He was the Beckham of his generation, although rather less well-paid, and no doubt Billy Wright would have travelled regularly by Midland Red when he was growing up, whatever transport he became used to later.

I determined to repeat the 1956 bus journey to Wellington. This I did, although inevitably with variations, the whole area now being part of the Borough of Telford & Wrekin. If I had asked for a ticket to said place in 1956 I would have received a very blank look from the conductor. The Wrekin, yes, for this is a prominent hill beside Wellington, and during the war I could look out of my aunt's upstairs window at night and see its aircraft warning light shining far away at its summit.

Modern Telford lies at the heart of the collection of small towns and villages between the Gorge and the A5 and the M54, and nearly all the local bus services call at its substantial bus station. The less said the better about its rail station, which, along with its car park, is totally inadequate for the business it does. Wellington station, although no longer served by any branches, retains most of its original buildings and is far better.

Wellington bus station is adequate, although a lot less busy than Telford's, and its bus garage is still in Charlton Street. At weekends in the 1950s nearly all bus crews attended church several times a day — or so one must assume, for one seldom saw a bus out and about on the Sabbath. It is not quite the same now, and to cater for the visitors who flock to the Ironbridge Experience every weekend throughout the year two services, WH1 and WH2, are operated by Choice Travel of Willenhall. The WH1 runs some dozen return journeys from Coalport China Museum via Blists Hill Victorian Town, Madeley bus station (where it connects with other routes), the Iron bridge, along the east bank of the Severn to the Museum of the Gorge, and then up the valley to Coalbrookdale Museum of Iron and a new feature for children called Enginuity. The WH2 does four circular trips from Much Wenlock to Buildwas Abbey, Ironbridge and along the Severn, and then back by way of Jackfield Tile Museum and Broseley.

Arriva Midlands, successor to Midland Red, remains the dominant provider of public transport in the area. The old route numbers — in the 9xx series for the Shrewsbury and Wellington areas, with 8xxs coming from the Stafford and Wolverhampton directions — have gone, and I boarded the first 76 of the day for the 52-minute run to Wellington.

Left: **Fast-forward to the late 1990s, and Shrewsbury is served by Midland Red North, whose fleet includes Mercedes-Benz minibuses which some might view as the antithesis of the proud engineering heritage of the company's mighty predecessor. This Merc has a Carlyle body.**
Stewart J. Brown

Right: **At Ironbridge — the famous structure is behind the photographer — a Plaxton-bodied Dennis Dart SLF operated by Elcock of Madeley heads towards Telford on the 96 service from Shrewsbury.**
Stewart J. Brown

Left: **Also linking Shrewsbury with Telford was the Midland Red North X5, operated in the late 1990s by a Leyland Tiger with Duple 340 body.**
Stewart J. Brown

Right: **Today the Wellington-based fleet of Arriva contains Wright-bodied DAF SB200s, one of which is seen approaching the town centre in 2003.**
Stewart J. Brown

Right: **For a short period in the mid-1990s Midland Red North adopted a retro livery of all-over dark red with shaded gold 'MIDLAND' fleetnames, as seen on this Wellington-bound Dennis Falcon with East Lancs body.**
Stewart J. Brown

Fourteen DAF SB200s with Wright Commander bodies were delivered to Wellington garage in 2002, and these operate many of the Telford services. Amongst other types are some Mini Pointer Darts and one of these sat in the rain waiting for me opposite the famous bridge (although the timetable records the starting point as the Tontine public house). And only me, it seemed. I offered the driver a fiver, which didn't go down too well, so popped across the road for a paper and change, and, good relations restored, we sat until precisely 08.40, when off we went: alongside the Severn to the Museum of the Gorge and then away up the valley to the Museum of Iron, passing immediately beforehand a works still producing iron goods, as it has been for 200 years — is there a rival anywhere in the world to equal this record? Having turned under the railway viaduct which carries coal trains to and from Buildwas power station (whose giant cooling towers on the banks of the Severn are as dramatic in their late-20th-century way as is the iron bridge), we climbed up a narrow lane overhung by trees sporting their very best autumn colours, reversed in a small, modern, rather exclusive-looking estate of houses and came back down again — still just the bus, the driver and me.

At the bottom of the hill, by the youth hostel, we were joined by a second passenger, with a large backpack. Gradually the Dart began to take on a sizeable load, darting (oops, sorry!) here and there in and out of country lanes, former mining villages and settlements, rows of red brick 19th-century terraces, interspersed with late-20th-century developments.

Now we were doing excellent business. Nearly everyone seemed to know everyone else, including Mary, who warned Alf to 'Go steady up the stairs' as he alighted and headed for his house a couple of doors up from China City — guess what delicacies you could buy there.

Amongst the damp attractions of Dawley were a 'Funeral Director for the Generations' and a local newspaper headline — 'Gazza in Telford' — about Paul Gascoigne (not quite the successor to Billy Wright), who had just returned from China (lucky the China City was handy) and signed for Wolves, expressing the somewhat forlorn hope that he might yet return to Premiership football. Eventually we pulled into Telford bus station, where plenty of Darts and DAFs, 11 in all, were loading and unloading. Sixteen passengers got out. Just one got in.

A couple of minutes wait produced no further business and off we went, getting up speed, the last section of the journey belting along a rural main road to Wellington station, with a DMU in the bay platform and the bus station and journey's end next door.

Arriva, Mini Pointer Darts and DMUs — all very different from Midland Red, SONs and steam-operated branch lines.

THE ALSO-RANS

All new models are launched by their makers with great hopes, but not all live up to expectations. *Stewart J. Brown* looks at some of those which have faltered in recent years.

All photographs by the author

Manufacturers launch new models with great optimism. They've done the market research — or so they would have you believe — and the latest model is what every bus or coach operator wants.

Sometimes it's true. When Dennis launched the Dart in 1988 as an improvement on van-derived minibuses no one at Guildford could have foreseen that it would propel Dennis to UK market leadership and establish the company in markets around the world, even if many of those markets proved difficult to develop.

Although, of course, the Dart wasn't Dennis's first foray into the midibus market. Two years before the Dart Dennis did build another midi, the Domino. This was a much heavier vehicle and only 34 were built with 20 going to Greater Manchester and 14 to South Yorkshire.

However, for every model which succeeds, there are many which fail, some quite spectacularly.

Take the Iveco TurboCity 100, a model which the Italian manufacturer said would become of major importance in the UK. At its launch in 1991 Iveco even put a figure on its impending success. It would, said the company, achieve 480 sales in the UK in five years.

In the end sales fell short of Iveco's target by a dramatic 479 vehicles. Only one TurboCity 100 was sold, and that was a bus which had been built as a demonstrator. It was, appropriately, painted white. As in white elephant.

The TurboCity 100 had a modified Alexander R-type body which incorporated Iveco's standard front end — rather as East Lancs would do 12 years later with the Scania-based OmniDekka. It was a 97-passenger bus, so the TurboCity 100 name used a bit of poetic licence. But, as so often happens with compromise designs which are adapted for new uses, the TurboCity 100 suffered from being based on an Italian single-deck chassis. The key dimensions were all wrong — for example, it had a rear overhang of almost 3m, compared with

2.35m on an Olympian — and the driveline layout meant there was a lot of wasted space around the rear of both saloons. Potential plus-points were independent front suspension and front disc brakes.

But two plus points do not a sales success make. The TurboCity 100 was an heroic failure.

The single-deck version — the TurboCity 50 — was unveiled in 1992 and did just a little better. A prototype was built with a two-door Alexander PS body, and Iveco then had a batch of six built for stock, this time bodied by Wadham Stringer. There were no queues of would-be buyers, and the TurboCitys found homes — no doubt at knock-down prices — with various small operators.

In 1998 Iveco was back in the single-deck bus business with the EuroRider. It sold one, with a Marshall body, to Whitelaw of Stonehouse. And in 2003, now as Irisbus, it was back again with the Agora Line, a joint venture with Optare, and with the Unvi-bodied MidiRider SLF. This time there were no wild sales forecasts.

At least Iveco could take satisfaction, albeit not very much, in the knowledge that one TurboCity 100 double-decker did actually enter revenue-earning service. That's more than can be said for Volvo's original low-floor double-decker, the B7L. This, like the Iveco, was built on a chassis designed for operation as a single-deck bus in mainland Europe. And once again the dimensions were all wrong, its overall length — and its long rear overhang — being out of step with the needs of UK fleets.

Even worse, the engine was mounted vertically in the rear nearside corner, taking up space which was badly needed for seats.

The one good thing about the B7L was its body, the first example of Plaxton's new President, which went on to become a significant success on a range of other chassis — including, in due course, the transverse-engined Volvo B7TL, which was the bus Volvo should have built for the UK in the first place.

The B7L cost Volvo dearly. In the days of the Olympian annual sales of Dennis double-deckers

were minimal. But the B7L was so obviously the wrong bus — and Dennis's competing Trident so obviously the right one — that Volvo double-deck buyers switched from Olympians to the new Dennis model. For proof just look at Stagecoach, Lothian and a host of London operators who would never have considered buying a Dennis Dominator but now run large fleets of Tridents.

Volvo did continue with the B7L as a single-decker, and, while it has sold in large numbers, primarily to FirstGroup, it has also been received with less enthusiasm by many other fleets, who switched to rival models — particularly from Scania — while Volvo's designers rushed back to their drawing boards to produce the B7RLE. This has its engine under the back seat, rather than in what has become known as the wardrobe in the corner, as on the B7L.

The B7L's predecessor — the B10L with Alexander Ultra body — was not an outstanding success either, even when Volvo made the chassis available to Wright to widen its appeal. The only big B10L users were Travel West Midlands, Ulsterbus and, with articulated B10LAs, FirstGroup.

Another low-floor body which did not achieve the successes it should have came from Northern Counties. Over the years its single-deck products have generally been less pleasing to the eye than its double-deckers, but the new Paladin, a surprise launch at the 1995 Coach & Bus Show, was a stylish design. Initially offered on the DAF SB220, a few were also built on Volvo's B10BLE, which had superseded the B10L.

The first few Paladins were built at Northern Counties' Wigan plant, but production was soon switched to Plaxton at Scarborough, and the model rebranded as the Plaxton Prestige. Presumably Plaxton hoped no-one would remember that the Prestige name had been coined just a few years earlier for an unsuccessful 3.7m-high export version of the Excalibur coach. The new Prestige bus did rather better than its namesake, but even so production only just made it into treble figures, almost all on DAF chassis. The biggest user was Arriva.

The Dart has been a tremendous success for Dennis, but other models of the 1980s fared less well. Fewer than 50 Lancet coaches were sold between 1981 and the end of production in 1988. The Lance bus chassis sold in reasonable numbers — some 500 in the UK — but when Dennis developed the Lance as a double-decker in 1995 and renamed it the Arrow it did less well. Only 75 had been built when production ended in 1998, with 56 of these going to one operator, Capital Citybus.

Earlier Dennis disasters included the rear-engined Falcon. It sold in moderate numbers as a single-deck bus — around 100 to UK operators — although when offered as a coach found just one buyer, NBC, which took 10. The double-deck version fared even less well, with only six built — three for

Right: **Most Plaxton Prestige bodies were on DAF SB220 chassis, but a small batch for Stagecoach were on Volvo's B10BLE. They were initially based in Manchester.**

Left: **A DAF SB220 with Plaxton Prestige body in the County Bus & Coach fleet. County took coach-seated Prestiges for the Green Line 724 service from Harlow to Heathrow.**

Right: **While Dennis's single-deck Lance sold in healthy numbers, the double-deck equivalent, the Arrow, was much less successful. The biggest user was Capital Citybus. This one has an East Lancs Pyoneer body.**

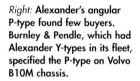

Greater Manchester, two for Nottingham and a Dennis demonstrator which nobody wanted to buy and which was sold off for use as a playbus.

Big manufacturers can get it wrong too, and in global bus terms they don't come much bigger than Mercedes-Benz. The German manufacturer announced a no-frills bus in 1995, the steel-suspended rear-engined OH1416 Urbanranger with attractive Wright body. It planned to sell 50 a year, but managed fewer than 15 in total.

Alexander's PS-type was a considerable success in the early 1990s, which overshadows the fact that as originally conceived it was a considerable failure. The P-type entered production in 1983 as the successor to the legendary Y-type bus. It was angular in appearance and had flat-glass

windscreens, Alexander's aim being to produce an easily-repairable body for export markets.

Original P-types found but a few buyers. Two Scottish Bus Group companies took 30 between them — 25 Leyland Tigers for Fife and Northern and five Dennis Lancets for Northern. South of the border buyers included Grimsby-Cleethorpes Transport and East Midland Motor Services (Tiger) and Badgerline, Burnley & Pendle and West Midlands Travel (Volvo B10M).

But when it was redesigned for Singapore — hence the 'S' in 'PS' — it was an altogether more attractive vehicle and was built on both mid- and rear-engined chassis for a range of British operators, including Stagecoach, Mainline in Sheffield and Busways in Newcastle, and even

Left: After buying almost 2,000 Alexander Y-types, a mere 30 P-types joined Scottish Bus Group fleets. The first were on Dennis Lancet chassis for Alexander (Northern).

Below: A novel feature of the Alexander P-type was the deep corner glass, designed to give the driver a better view of the kerb and clearly visible on this Grimsby-Cleethorpes Leyland Tiger.

Left: Before standardising on the Leyland Lynx, West Midlands Travel evaluated a trial batch of six alongside a similar number of Volvo B10Ms with Alexander P-type bodies.

Above: The Scottish Bus Group's first Leyland Lions were delivered to Eastern Scottish in 1986. They had Alexander R-type bodies. This one is seen after Eastern Scottish had adopted SMT as its trading name and had been acquired by FirstBus.

Below: Nottingham City Transport had 13 Lions — an inauspicious number, some might say. The last five, delivered in 1989, had 88-seat East Lancs bodies.

Above: The Leyland Tiger Cub was a popular chassis in the 1950s and early 1960s, and Leyland no doubt hoped its new DAB-based Tiger Cub would be similarly successful in the 1980s. It wasn't. Only two were built, and they spent most of their lives in the immaculate fleet of Jim Stones of Leigh.

Left: The Leyland Swift had a vertical mid-mounted Cummins engine. This example, with Reeve Burgess Harrier body, was one of a pair for Pennine Motor Services of Gargrave.

entered service in London, on Dennis Lances for Selkent in pre-Stagecoach days.

The B10M, one of the most successful coach chassis of all time, was used by Volvo as the basis of the successful mid-engined Citybus double-decker. It was a shrewd move, dictated by Volvo's desire to sell what it could build, rather than developing a new design to meet the peculiar needs of Britain's double-deck buyers. And it panicked Leyland into a response with the Lion, based on a Danish-built DAB underframe. Only 32 Lions were sold.

Leyland also turned to its DAB subsidiary in the 1980s for a new breed of midibus, named the Tiger Cub. The plan was to import part-completed shells which would be finished and trimmed at the ECW factory in Lowestoft. Two were built, and it was left to Dennis to show what a midibus should really be like. The Tiger Cub was followed by the mid-engined

Right: **A small number of Leyland Swifts had Portuguese Elme bodies, including this example in the Cunningham Carriage Company fleet.**

Left: **Wright's Handybus body was not the company's most attractive product, and the extra height which it gained when mounted on a high-frame Leyland Swift rather than on a Dennis Dart did nothing to improve its looks. This Arriva Swift started life with Stevensons of Uttoxeter.**

Right: **The ugliest Swift of all? The ugliest bus of all time? PMT Knype bodywork was fitted to a few Swifts, including this example in the Crosville fleet, complete with corporate FirstBus logo.**

Swift, which sold in small numbers, normally with bodywork by Reeve Burgess or Wadham Stringer. It used the same engine and gearbox as the Dart, but Dennis had the right configuration where Leyland got it wrong.

Inspired by the success of the Dart, other manufacturers developed models to try to win a share of Britain's booming midibus business. Volvo's intermittent success with the B6R, B6LE and B6BLE in its various guises was overshadowed by the small Dennis, while other manufacturers stood no chance at all.

Remember the Cannon? Northern Ireland manufacturer Cannon exhibited a Dart-like chassis at various events, but both chassis and builder quietly disappeared. Cannon also developed a small mid-engined chassis, but the number built for coach operation failed to reach double figures, although it had a little more success in the welfare market.

Marshall was another manufacturer with an eye on the midibus market. Based in Cambridge, the company had over the years taken a greater or lesser interest in building bus bodies, depending, one suspects, on whether it had other more lucrative aircraft or military contracts to keep its

workforce busy. It had been a big supplier to the BET group in the 1960s and built double-deck bodies in the late 1970s and early 1980s, buyers including the Derby, Leicester and Newport municipal fleets and South Yorkshire PTE. It worked with Bedford to develop the stylish and innovative JJL minibus in the mid-1970s — truly a bus ahead of its time — and it was also a long-term supplier of utilitarian bus bodies to the Ministry of Defence.

In 1992 Marshall took over the design rights to the Dart body being built by Carlyle, which had in turn taken it over from Duple. An interesting side-effect of this, incidentally, was the production by Marshall of 20 Dart-style bodies on the rival Volvo B6R chassis for Cambus and Bebb's of South Wales.

Anyway, Marshall developed an improved midibus body, built on Dennis and MAN chassis, and then decided there was room in the market for a smaller vehicle. Thus was born the integral Marshall Minibus. On paper it looked great — a compact bus with a Cummins/Allison drivetrain. The Cummins engine was a four-cylinder version of the six-cylinder unit used by Dennis in the Dart.

But what looked good on paper proved unreliable in service. Deliveries were slow, and a Mk 2 version was produced in 1997 to address the failings of the original model, but to no avail. The two big buyers of Marshall Minibuses — London General and CentreWest — returned them to Marshall and

Below: **The Marshall Minibus was a spectacular failure and those bought by London operators were soon sold on to new owners, including Buzz Bus in Harlow.**

Above: **The UK's first modern low-floor buses came from Neoplan and were for operation on Merseyside. Neoplan buses in Arriva livery are rare indeed.**

replaced them with Darts. Marshall did manage to resell the Minibuses, but by this time everyone knew their reputation and no doubt paid a price which reflected this.

Marshall, of course, is no more, although its spirit lives on in the MCV business, which is building a Marshall-style body in small numbers in a factory in Cambridgeshire.

Neoplan, which has been supplying coaches to British operators for some 25 years, has had little success with buses. Britain's first modern low-floor bus was a Neoplan which entered service with Merseyside Transport in 1993, the precursor of a fleet of 12 delivered in 1994. In 1997 Neoplan tried selling the Hungarian-built N4015 in the UK. A right-hand-drive vehicle was exhibited at that year's Coach & Bus show, but produced no orders.

Success and failure in the coach market is often more difficult to judge than in the bus business. Many manufacturers and importers are geared up to sell only small numbers and are happy if annual sales creep into double figures. So the fact that you don't see many of a particular model could be no more than a reflection of the modest aspirations of its dealer or manufacturer.

Over the years there have been many examples

of what are known in the trade as 'one-season wonders' — models which arrive with a great fanfare and then disappear, typically after a couple of seasons.

Back in the 1980s and early 1990s there were the TAZ Dubrava and the FAP Famos, cheap imports from Eastern Europe. They were often bought by small coach operators who were attracted by the prestige of having a new coach but couldn't afford mainstream models such as the B10M/Van Hool or Tiger/Plaxton. Coach bodies which have come and gone in the last two decades, leaving no lasting impact, have included Ajokki, Elme, Hispano, Obradors, OVI, Padane, Smit and Van Rooijen.

Macedonian builder MCI threatened to take the coach industry by storm, promising a whole range of models at the start of the 2000s, buses included. In the event the only MCI products to reach these shores were rebodies on Volvo chassis for Dunn-Line of Nottingham.

Hispano bodied the Vita coach for Mercedes-Benz in 1997 and more recently has been chosen by Volvo to body the B7L citybus, as an alternative to the popular Wrightbus Eclipse body. With the B7L's poor reception in the market the B7L/Hispano is a combination which would seem to be doomed from the start, even with Volvo offering it in both 12m rigid and 18m articulated versions.

There's a lot of hyperbole surrounding the launch of a new model. History shows that it often has to be taken with a pinch of salt.

Right: Italian-built Padane bodies were imported to the UK for a short period in the early 1980s and had distinctive styling, which is obscured by the unsympathetic application of Scottish Citylink colours on this Volvo B10M operated by Dodds of Troon.

Left: Whose body is this? Top marks if you identified it as one of the few Smits sold in Britain. It's on a DAF SB2300 chassis.

Right: It might look like a Mercedes, but it is in fact a Yugoslavian-built FAP Famos. The badge on the front shows it's not a Merc, although some buyers replaced the Yugoslavian manufacturer's emblem with the rather more prestigious three-pointed star. The FAP Famos was marketed in the UK as the Ensign Charisma.

HIGH CAPACITY

While midibuses of various sizes have dominated new bus deliveries in recent years, there are now significant numbers of high-capacity buses entering service. *David Barrow* illustrates some recent examples.

Above: **Brighton & Hove favoured Scanias right from the start of its existence as a private-sector business, buying its first in 1988. It returned to the marque in 2003, taking 18 Scania/ East Lancs OmniDekkas, with a further 18 following in 2004. Two of the 2003 vehicles are seen in the centre of Brighton.**

Left: **Included in the Brighton & Hove 2003 OmniDekka order were a pair of convertible open-toppers, one of which is seen at Devil's Dyke.**

Above: Metrobus, like Brighton & Hove, is part of Go-Ahead Group, and it too operates OmniDekkas, including some of the first to be built. The colourful livery is an imaginative approach to Transport for London's requirement that buses on London contracts should be predominantly red. The Metrobus OmniDekka is red but relieved by Metrobus's traditional colours of blue and yellow. This is Croydon.

Below: Wrightbus has made an impression amongst buyers of double-deckers with its striking Eclipse Gemini on Volvo's B7TL chassis. Travel West Midlands was the first user of the model outside London, taking 60 in 2003 and a further 70 in 2004.

Above: Nottingham City Transport took 23 OmniDekkas in 2003. This view shows the clean lines of the East Lancs body with just four main side windows — all the same size — on the upper deck. The front dash panel is of a Scania design and is used on other members of the Omni family. The Nottingham OmniDekkas are 12m long.

Left: Most new Stagecoach double-deckers have had bodywork built in Falkirk by Alexander or TransBus. But in 2003 Stagecoach took 40 Wigan-built TransBus Presidents, most of which were for service in Greater Manchester. The chassis were long-wheelbase TransBus Tridents, the added length in the body being made up using a short window in mid-wheelbase.

Right: A standard-length Trident/President delivered to Metroline in 2003. Metroline was one of the first users of the President in 1999, when it was still a Plaxton product. This one is at Brent Cross shopping centre.

Right: Mayne of Manchester switched from East Lancs to TransBus for the bodywork on two Tridents delivered in 2003. These were 100-passenger buses, with 78 seats and space for 22 standees. A First Manchester articulated Volvo can be seen in the background in this view in Manchester city centre.

Above: Articulated buses have appeared in service in significant numbers since 2002, mostly in London, and most of them Mercedes-Benz Citaros. This 2003 Stagecoach London example is approaching Westminster Bridge and is in the shadow of Big Ben. Arriva, Go-Ahead and FirstGroup also run Citaro artics in the capital.

Right: Interest in artics outside London has been limited. FirstGroup has a number of Wright-bodied Volvos, while Travel West Midlands has two generations of Mercedes, the newest, delivered in 2003, being 10 dual-door Citaros in Travel Coventry colours.

Above: Blackpool Transport's low-floor double-deckers are all Tridents with 77-seat East Lancs Lolyne bodies. There are 18, most of which carry green-and-yellow branding for Metro Line 14. This is a spare vehicle, in a black-and-yellow livery, and in place of route-specific details on the side appears the message 'Every Day, All Day, Reliable, Frequent'.

Below: A major coup for Wrightbus was securing orders from FirstGroup for its Eclipse Gemini bodywork, with over 100 being delivered in the winter of 2003/4. The first examples went to Sheffield. Later deliveries were for London (in red, of course) and Leeds.

WORDS UPON THE FINE ART of BUS PHOTOGRAPHY

(or How Not to be Hit by a Handbag)

With this essay *Robert E. Jowitt* will doubtless infuriate some readers, delight others and while retaining a firmly 1960s attitude to the subject may yet in 2004 provide some helpful hints …

All photographs by the author

The most depressing article — and set of photographs — that it was ever my misfortune to study dealt with the subject of how to photograph a bus. I no longer recall who brought this dire item to my attention, nor who wrote it, nor in what journal it appeared, so I can be as rude as I like about it without risk of being sued.

But I won't be. Let's just say the writer took a series of photographs of buses in sundry locations but you couldn't tell where they were anyway; each photo was trimmed as close to the bus as possible and each photo had a background of something like Woolworth or WHS in such space as was allowed behind the bus.

Chacun à son goût — everyone has his or her own taste of how to photograph a bus (or anything else, come to that), so I will here just set down, because our excellent editor has been kind enough to allow me space to do so, my own opinions on the subject.

In truth I would not care to be a photographer of buses. My real affections, as I have stated perhaps too often in the pages of *Buses Yearbook*, lie with steam or electric narrow-gauge railways or, come to that, standard-gauge railways (but life's best pleasures pass away all too fast, with 'West Country' Pacifics and Portuguese Henschell Mallet 0-4-4-0s all dead and gone) or elderly electric trams

Below left: **Classic totally boring three-quarter-front view, here in 1964 of equally classic SHMD Daimler CVD6 with Northern Counties body.**

Right: **Utterly boring shot of coach from the Isle of Mull on the Isle of Wight. The coach is a Neoplan Skyliner belonging to Essbee.**

Left: **Buses at right-angles generally form a good theme, although in this 1998 Edinburgh shot there are too many cars and vans, and the statue appears to be riding atop a bus.**

such as you could formerly encounter in Glasgow or Lisbon or the Fatherland, or even trolleybuses, but not buses, no, except for real classics such as the famous Parisian Renault TNs and (though rather less so) the famous French pig-snout Chaussons or the AECs in Lisbon … but then, because there is nothing else around (except a few fairly modern and fairly nasty trolleybuses in faraway foreign places) I find myself dragged into fancying such dreadful vehicles as the Saviem SC10 or the Leyland Olympian.

Anyway, however dreadful the buses may be, the compulsion is there, just to photograph them.

But *not* from three-quarters front with a close-cropped backdrop of Woollies.

No. However, as *malgré moi* or, to put it not in French, in spite of myself I have become a bus

photographer with works frequently accepted by such notable editors as those of *Buses Yearbook…* and *Classic Bus Yearbook*, come to that … and regardless of obloquy heaped upon my style from certain quarters — and almost certainly from the worthy gent mentioned above — I now describe with a few helpful hints and so forth how and why I go about the business …

If you really want to photograph a bus by itself, from three-quarter front or from any other aspect, forget about Woollies and WHS; try to catch the creature in a totally empty space such as an airfield or a housing estate which hasn't yet been built. Possibly, in the latter case, try to ornament the picture with one lone lovely tree which the ideal-home-builders have so far neglected to cut down. But be careful here. I once (actually more than

once) was called upon to act as judge of the photographic contributions of the Southampton University Transport Society (an institution which, sad to relate, no longer exists, save as an occasional reunion of the 'old boys', though whether this indicates the boringness of modern transport or decay in university students' tastes I cannot say) and severely took to task one of these brave fellows who had produced a photo of some type of open-topper in front of some fir trees; unfortunately for him and his position the bus appeared to be sprouting the fir trees from its upper deck, and for months afterwards the members of the 'Transoc', so I was told, were wont to mutter to each other when out on their forays 'Beware of Christmas trees growing on the top deck!'

By the same token, dare I add, I once took issue with that renowned bus photographer Ian Cowley for his efforts on a Leyland National boasting a splendid Gothic chapel as its upper deck. I am pleased to say that despite this attack we have remained good friends. And while still complaining on this topic I must make mention of the fact that even such eagle-eyed editors as Booth and Brown (of *CBY* and *BY* respectively) allow now and then to slip into their pages a handsome-looking bus which would give a visitor from Mars (or even somewhere nearer, perhaps) the impression that the vehicle must contain several fireplaces for there are several delectable Victorian chimney-pots poking out from its roof. I hope, of course, that regardless of this

criticism I shall continue to remain equally good friends with Messrs B and B.

While avoiding chimneys and Christmas trees on the roof another dire warning becomes necessary, especially to the faithful few who consider that black-and-white is best. To this truth I have myself always been devout, being well kicked into it in my youth when no editor would touch colour unless submitted in 2¼in-square transparency format and even then only rarely, and the cost of colour-neg developing and printing was fairly prohibitive and not editorially acceptable … to which I have to add and admit that in recent years with cheap offers of colour d&p coming through the letter box nearly every other day and the effort involved in b&w printing on contemporary buses, many of which in my eyes hardly deserve such time and trouble, I have come to a compromise with my conscience and tend to settle for cheapo-color; and before I return to my dire warning — which is to some extent relevant even with cheapo-color — I must firmly state that I will never sink to a digital camera or computerised messing-about …

… pause for breath after delivery of one of those lengthy sentences which editors seem to regard as the cream of my literary endeavour …

I have yet to see results from digital cameras which match up to the best results of traditional cameras, though I can foresee that, even if at great expense, such a day may come … and the darkroom become a legend of ancient history. I, however, shall remain in the Dark Ages, and if i want to fiddle with *montages* I will do so with two enlargers side by side, with marked baseboards and wasting a lot of paper on 'test-strips'. (A newspaper reporter from Canada was sufficiently impressed by a picture I had thus achieved that he requested a 20in copy to hang in his living-room — another paper-wasting but fulfilling day for Robert E. Jowitt in the darkroom!) And if the shots need 'bleeding in' or even the odd chimney pot removed I will achieve the necessary result under the enlarger-lens with moving hands or pieces of cardboard or Kleenex tissue. Which brings me back to the dire warning threatened above.

Beware of the bus with white or cream roof. It is not a serious problem in city streets with high buildings where sooty architecture forms an edge to the top, but in wide open spaces the blend of pale sky and light roof can leave the bus with nothing but the bland heavens above the tops of the windows … or nothing without tedious under-enlarger toil! Therefore set your pale-roofed bus against a dark background … but, returning to Square One, don't let it look as if trees … or chapels … or chimneys … are part of Duple's or Plaxton's creation.

Another interesting method of coping with the bus just as bus is to go up into a high place — an excellent habit much practised by prophets in the pages of Holy Writ — such as the top of a multi-storey car-park or the fifth floor in a Portuguese

Above: **Architecturally speaking, the composition must contain as much of the building as possible, as seen here with what appears to be a non-conformist chapel on the Scilly Isles with coaches of Austin and Bedford manufacture.**

slum (not, of course, that either of these features in Holy Writ) and shoot down; and if you are really lucky you will end up with just the roof, and it doesn't matter in this case if it is pale, and anyway you will produce some unusual distortions!

Turning, however, from the photo of the bus by itself (which was what the above paragraphs were about, let me remind you) I hold the view that the bus is not normally by itself; on the contrary, it is part of a scene, a vibrant and probably noisy part of a scene — and incidentally as a part of that scene it is only for a few seconds that it plays its role as three-quarters from the front, for first it is a speck in the distance and then not much later it is roaring broadside-on past you and then it is the celebrated (if little photographed) 'back end of a bus' and then it is a speck in the opposite distance — while the scene itself may be a crowded city street or a lane in some mountainous fastness or any other location you may fancy … so the appeal to me is to put the bus in this scene with all the surrounding human life and all the architecture or all the loneliness or whatever options are on offer (though not, if I can avoid it, WHS or Woollies …).

Of all the surrounding human life the most charming aspect to me is the girls on the pavements, and I may claim that I am widely renowned — and probably equally reviled (in some quarters) — for my fashion of not caring if this miniskirt or that pair of tight jeans occludes some precious detail such as the number-plate of the bus.

Above: **The back of a Hampshire Bus Bristol VRT slips charmingly into a side street in Winchester. The equally charming girl on the right has a one-way sign growing from her curly locks.**

The latest fashion in tight jeans, and one to which I ought obviously to turn my attention in connection with buses in the proximity, seems to include a midriff or degree of unclad stomach regardless of climatic inclemency, which borders almost, by the low line of what might be called the waist, on what might be termed as indecency. This is evidently something on which I must concentrate my lens if I can bear the frostbite which must equally health-wise be damaging these poor girls' lusts for high fashion.

But to turn from such display I could add that I am just as undismayed if it happens to be a picturesque old-age pensioner or senior citizen or tramp or hippie who fouls the number-plate, but I have to admit that the insertion of a charming damsel pleases me best. I have frequently been asked, over four decades in this pursuit, how often have I been hit by the girls I photographed. The answer is never; the only time I have been hit by a girl I was trying to photograph was more than four decades ago: we went to the same dancing class and I really fancied her and she knew I wanted to take her photograph and she didn't want me to and one day I saw her coming up the High Street, Winchester, and started firing on my Ilford Sportsman and she charged at me and really clouted me with her handbag … and there wasn't a bus in sight, the nearest were King Alfred PD2s right down at the bottom of the High Street. Dear Susan … Later (a couple of years) I managed to get a shot of her at a respectable teenage charity ball, but since then (what a pity!) I have quite lost track of her. So, no, I have not been attacked by any of these maidens whose likeness it has been my pleasure to record with diverse buses behind them.

I think (if I dare divulge it) that the secret of the art is this. You see the bus and the girl coming more or less side-by-side, and you shoot the pair, and then you go on looking at the bus and shooting or at least pretending to shoot the bus, so the girl just thinks 'gricer' (or whatever her abusive term for a bus-photographer may be …) and passes on without a threatening twitch of handbag. Maybe you miss a lot of interesting dates this way, but you don't get hit and you do have the photo. Nevertheless I encountered three places where the rule didn't seem to apply, namely Lisboa, Porto and Edinburgh, where girls, singly or in groups, saw exactly what I was doing and then wanted to be photographed anyway, never mind that there was no bus or tram in sight behind. Not that this, lovely as they all were, got me any dates either …

And then I have to say that even the most beautiful girl, as you snatch a brief glimpse of her in all her charm — pre-Raphaelite or Renoir or any other as the seconds may reveal it — is not so easy to record. If she is with a girl friend they will both be gossiping, probably not listening to each other but their mouths both open; if it is in the declining evening sun and the buses are looking their best and out in force (*q.v.* hereinafter) she will either be squinting horribly against the light or her face and all the rest of her will be in total darkness. I would guess that out of hundreds or probably even thousands of shots I have taken in this vein only a

Above: **Five lovely ladies dancing at Epsom in the 1980s, with a Plaxton Paramount as a backdrop to show the problem of a pale roof against a pale sky.**

Right: **There's something threatening about a tilting bus. This is Hampshire Bus VR YEL 1T with three ladies in Winchester.**

very few per cent of them actually do true justice to the maids involved … but of course that few per cent makes the game worth the candle.

Senior citizens are easier — though I do not want to be accused of 'ageism' — but it doesn't seem to matter if they are cross-eyed or scowling or even gossiping … and gossiping is surely one of the greatest pleasures of senior citizens … and then architecture is easier still … always provided that you handle it right and don't get a Gothic chapel as top deck for a National! Without reference to some excellent tome such as *The Little Red Book* (which research I do not propose to undertake) I cannot answer the question which I am asking myself, namely whether there are more urban or more rural buses in everyday service, though I would imagine the answer must favour the former.

If such is the case, urban architecture must play a vital part in a large proportion of bus photographs, in every degree from the humble slum terrace awaiting demolition and the notably ornate Victorian gin-palace to the greatest cathedral. And to pay adequate attention to such surroundings … well, for example, the spire of Salisbury Cathedral, the tallest in England, is 404ft tall, the bus is not much

above 14ft tall, to do justice to both the bus might end up covering only ten percent of the picture, but you do see where your bus is. If you can't contain the whole building in your shot then at least try to trim it according to architectural decency, use a string-course or some other recognisable feature for the top of the frame; don't have the bottom half of a window seeping in if you can possibly avoid it.

Then out and about with the (presumed) smaller percentage of rural buses, even here you have

Above: **Rare medieval strip cultivation and 18th-century quarries on the Isle of Portland with a Bristol VR, all photographed from the deck of the preserved Clyde paddle-steamer** *Waverley.*

Below: **A Hampshire Bus Leyland National passing Itchen water meadows at St Catherine's Down, near Winchester, in 1984.**

architecture because the buses wouldn't be there if they weren't on their way to villages (except if they were doing the inter-urban trip) and village vernacular can furnish a great deal of information on the bus story. As for the empty spaces between the villages, be they the upland wilds of the Pennines or the flat eternity of the Fens, if you do not include a considerable portion of wild upland or eternal flatness in your picture you might as well be back on the aerodrome or the unbuilt housing estate.

Back to the bus just as a bus.

Now if the need arises where I have to photograph a bus just as a bus — and it has to be a pretty exciting bus for me to engage in such endeavour or else something really bizarre like a much-mutilated Hippie-bus — I would far sooner shoot it broadside-on, a pose regarded (though goodness knows why) with some abhorrence by the three-quarter-front gang, and, for preference with a panning-shot at speed. This for me captures the size, the spirit and the motion of the bus. I am not alone in this persuasion; Ian Cowley, as mentioned above — and despite his chapel — has achieved masterpieces in this vein, masterpieces of which I am deeply envious.

An attractive alternative to the broadside view is the absolutely head-on view, though obviously if the bus is in motion there is some risk attached to this style of shot, such as death … under the wheels of the thing you are trying to photograph. Fortunately (or perhaps otherwise in some people's view) this

fate has so far eluded me. The answer is to attack the creature on a bend or curve, so that for a moment you see it right straight-on head-first and you shoot it thus and then it moves on round the bend and doesn't actually crush you. If there happens to be another bus coming the other way (*i.e.* from behind you) — and if this doesn't run you over either while your attention is taken with the bus coming forwards — you may then achieve a very satisfactory shot with both the front of the oncoming bus and the rear of the other … or the famous 'back-end of a bus' as quoted above.

I must admit I do not understand why the back end of the bus suffers so much obloquy in common parlance. Well, for a truth, nowadays certain backsides with all-over adverts are fairly horrible, but in the joyous days of my youth the rear platform of a Parisian Renault TN or a London Transport RT or RM made as pretty a picture as you could wish to see … especially if there was a charming girl on the step …

Leaving the girl — reluctantly — aside and continuing the theme of the bus by itself, well, if you are having a bus by itself, without girls or architecture, you might as well be extravagant and include as many buses as you can in the picture … Here I must turn to another master; Tom Moore is

surely the finest exponent of this *genre*, and if you search through earlier editions of *Buses Yearbook* or *Buses Annual* you will see exactly what I mean.

To elaborate on what I mean, there is a poem by the French poet Guillaume Apollinaire (1880-1918, regarded as a symbolist and surrealist) in his collection of verses on *Alcools* which dwells for five lines on a gin-inspired view of Paris tramways, and some of these lines are quoted in one of François Sagan's novels, and these lines are (in my view mistakenly) brought up to date in the English translation as 'herds of bellowing buses'. Nevertheless, 'herds of bellowing buses' is a fine phrase, and it is herds of bellowing buses which with neither the aid of architecture nor uplands or flatlands nor even girls can provide a marvellous kaleidoscopic pattern assembled simply from the ever-changing movements of their bellowing.

Try any point where buses gather together, a bus station or perhaps better the streets in the rush

hour, nose to tail and nose to tail or head-on with another broadside across the back, perhaps good with a telephoto lens but perhaps nearly as good on a standard and do a 'blow-up' afterwards, and you have nothing but bits of buses at various angles, and infinitely more artistic than the three-quarter-front with a tiny corner of Woollies.

The more buses the better, never mind that you can't read the number-plates, never mind what sort of buses they are, never mind the three-quarter-front attitude, just make the most of the herd.

Never mind that you are breaking all the rules of the seriously moral and upright traditionalists; for it may be the case that you are creating something really artistic.

Never mind either if by good luck some absolutely stunningly beautiful girl glides past to wreck and enhance the picture.

But if you approach the shot the wrong way and she hits you with her handbag, DON'T BLAME ME …

TWENTY YEARS OF
OPTARE

Amazingly 2005 sees Optare's 20th anniversary. *Stephen Morris* looks back at the roller-coaster ride of a company which, given the climate in which it was born, seemed doomed to instant failure.

If there was a business not to be in in the 1980s it was building buses. Not in Britain, anyway. The political climate certainly wasn't in favour of manufacturing industry in general. Prime Minister Margaret Thatcher was determined to build a new Britain in which everyone stood on their own two feet and in which manufacturing industry would give way to service industry.

Standing on our own two feet included the bus industry, from which as much subsidy would be driven out as possible. New Bus Grant, introduced under the 1968 Transport Act to help operators convert their services to one-person operation, was being phased out, doubling the price of a new bus, and the industry was to be fundamentally restructured. It might lead to a brave new future for the bus industry (and I leave it to you, dear reader, to decide whether or not we are now living in that brave future), but in the short term the future was so uncertain that only the brave or foolhardy would commit to buying new buses at double the price they had been not so long before.

It was against this background that in 1985 I was rendered incredulous by the decision of one man to start a new bus-building business in Leeds. Over the following years I got to know that man, Russell Richardson, and like most of us in or around the industry I have great respect for him as a man of vision and good sense. At the time I thought he was barking. Totally barking.

I first met Russell a couple of years or so earlier, when he was plant director of Leyland's Charles H. Roe bodybuilding factory at Cross Gates in Leeds. The press had been invited to Cross Gates to see in build a most un-Roe-like product — a batch of articulated buses on Leyland-DAB chassis for British Airways. This looked like a sort of highbridge, stretched Leyland National, being one of several spin-offs made possible by that bus's remarkably tough and versatile body structure, and parts were shipped across the Pennines from Workington for Roe to assemble. Workington was good at churning out standardised bodies, and Roe was good at doing more specialist things.

Downturn in demand for buses, industrial-relations problems and questions over Leyland's reliability in the face of Continental newcomers like Volvo, DAF and Scania — whose products quickly made Leyland's look dated — were all having their effect, and Leyland was busy shedding bus-building capacity. AEC and Park Royal had both gone in 1979, though some of Park Royal's previous output was met by increasing capacity at Workington, where the workforce was less intractable. At the time of my visit Roe's capacity was five double-deckers a week (or four and an artic), and soon it would be difficult to fill even that modest capacity. When Leyland introduced its new Royal Tiger Doyen coach in 1982, this was to be built at Leeds. It took quite some time to get production going, and it was soon decided to transfer most production to Workington, leaving Roe to build the more specialist variants. All the time Roe's double-deck output was declining; fewer than two double-deckers a week were emerging by 1984, and the writing was on the wall. Its last bus, a Leyland Olympian for local operator West Yorkshire PTE — 5145 (B140 RWY) — rolled out of the factory in September 1984, and the closure was marked with a gathering of Roe-bodied buses down the years on the 23rd of that month. There was still over-capacity in the industry, and that, surely, was the end of the road.

One institution to which Margaret Thatcher had not yet turned her attention was the Metropolitan counties (that would come later), and the West Yorkshire's Enterprise Board, together with Russell Richardson, who had already left Leyland and gone to Duple, quickly entered negotiations with Leyland to acquire the Cross Gates Carriage Works. West Yorkshire Enterprise Board bought the site and put it on a 20-year lease to a new company set up by Russell — Optare, whose strange name is Latin for 'to choose'.

Former Roe employees were invited to sink their redundancy pay into the new business, which at this stage amounted to little more than an empty shell, and 100 of them were taken back on. Some equipment was bought back from Leyland, including some digitally controlled precision tooling and a 240-ton press, but other items, such as a spray booth, had to be acquired separately.

The new business started on 15 February 1985 with a completely empty factory, but it did at least have an order book. Yorkshire's two Metropolitan counties had come up with backing for the new business, including orders for 14 midibuses based on the Dennis Domino chassis for South Yorkshire and 15 Leyland Olympians, to be bodied to the old Roe design, and 15 Leyland Cubs, with bodywork similar to that of South Yorkshire's Dominos, for West Yorkshire, with the promise of minibus work from the latter too.

Given that the company had started with a clean sheet on 15 February, it was no mean achievement when the first Domino for South Yorkshire emerged from the factory on 31 May the same year.

Over the years some very handsome products have emerged from Cross Gates, but it's probably true to say that South Yorkshire's Dominos were not amongst them. The best that could be said for their styling was that they had a certain rugged charm, and they at least looked better than essentially the same body for West Yorkshire on the Leyland Cub. South Yorkshire evidently had a major hand in the design, and they were quite clearly related to the Dennis Dominators it was then having bodied by Alexander, East Lancs and Northern Counties. The Dominos were 7.8m long and 2.3m wide, with 33 seats, and were solidly built in aluminium, fixed together with Leyland National-style Advelok adhesive bolts.

For much of its first year Optare was dependent on business from West Yorkshire PTE, which duly joined the deregulation minibus revolution by ordering 15 Freight Rover Sherpa parcel vans, to be converted into competent minibuses by Optare. West Yorkshire's ambulance service also got Optare to convert a Renault Master into an ambulance, and these obviously appealed to some of the ambulance services in the North East, as 38 were built around the turn of 1986/7, mostly for Northumbria but with six for Cleveland and eight for Durham. Leeds City Council also supported its new local enterprise, with two mobile libraries on Ford R1115 chassis and 12 welfare buses on Renault-Dodge S56 chassis.

Such work was certainly vital to Optare to get it off the ground, but reliance on work kindly provided

Below: **One of Optare's first orders was for Leyland-style bodies on Olympians for West Yorkshire PTE. Similar buses would go to Reading, Maidstone and Cambus.** *Stewart J. Brown*

by its local authority was not conducive to creating a thriving long-term business. Indeed, the abolition of the Metropolitan counties would probably have sounded Optare's death-knell had it not prepared itself to appeal to the wider world.

Optare's strength was in having an experienced workforce and yet not having the baggage of a long-established traditional company; this was to prove a potent combination, and it wasn't long before Optare started 'thinking outside the box', which, given the looks of the midibuses on Domino and Cub chassis, seems a particularly appropriate epithet.

Design talent was brought in from local colleges to produce the vehicle which was to set Optare apart from the common horde. The company was

able to persuade MAN-VW to produce a special version of its LT van chassis, a heavier-weight version than was otherwise available in the UK, the LT55, on which to build a 25-seater with room for around five standing. Moreover, MAN-VW authorised some fairly major modification of the chassis by Optare to suit it for its new role.

Although the market was still very much into 16-20-seat minibuses, Optare correctly foresaw a move to slightly larger vehicles, and it also judged that something rather better than the van-like styling of minibuses then on the road was needed. The result was the CityPacer, which, with its huge one-piece raked windscreen and attractive 'big bus' styling, was quite unlike anything else around at the time.

The VW was an untried chassis for the bus

market, and its six-cylinder 2.4-litre engine was smoother than other builders' four-cylinder units of similar capacity, but it was rather too small for a vehicle of its size and, with the CityPacer's smooth styling, unspoiled by grilles, tended to overheat. But it made operators sit up and take notice, and it sold well. In particular, one of its first customers was London Transport, which bought 52 to lease to operators. The CityPacer's sleek looks were just what it needed for a new experimental minibus service from Parliament Square through some of London's most fashionable bits — Belgravia, Sloane Square and Knightsbridge — to Kensington. However, these weren't London's first CityPacers, the first to enter service anywhere being five for Selkent's Roundabout network in Orpington.

Incredibly, Optare had come from a standing start to delivering its first CityPacer — a vehicle totally unlike anything seen before in the bus world — in just 12 months. The CityPacer was rewarded with the Gold Medal for coachwork at the 1986 Motor Show, at which appeared a coach version, the InterCityPacer. The wisdom at the time of deregulation was to buy vehicles at the price of £1,000 per seat, and a typical 16-seat Transit then cost £16,000. Despite its sophistication and style, the 25-seat CityPacer wasn't far off-beam, at £26,800 just short of £1,100 per seat. It was an instant hit being taken up by a number of minibus operators, including four local-authority fleets — Blackpool, which for a time used it as its standard minibus type, Leicester, which launched an attack

Above: **A new face for the '80s. A Leicester Citybus 'Trippit' Optare CityPacer in Loughborough in 1987.** *Adrian Pearson*

Left: **The CityPacer quickly took to the streets of London; this one, in a wet Kentish Town on 1 April 1987, was operated by London Country North West, though owned by LT.** *Kevin Lane*

on Loughborough with 11 smart green 'Trippit' examples, Southend, which had six, and Taff-Ely, which had seven. Yorkshire Rider and Cambus also took to the CityPacer, and more than 200 were on the road by the end of 1987.

Optare had plans to build up to 400 CityPacers a year but never got close to that figure. The model's best year was 1987, when 157 were built, and it tailed off rapidly after 1988, just 22 being built between 1989 and 1994. But the CityPacer had certainly succeeded in getting Optare on the map as a serious bus producer. It also established a principle that was rather different from the traditional way of building bus bodies in Britain: each Optare model was bespoke to one particular chassis and was marketed as an Optare product, not as a product of its chassis builder, and was entirely supported in the after-sales market as an Optare product.

Despite its stunning looks and passenger appeal, the CityPacer suffered from mechanical components which were just too lightweight for the job, and a larger model — the StarRider, based on the Mercedes 811D — soon followed. This lost something of the style of the CityPacer but produced a more acceptable 33-seater. Operators were rather less wary of the Mercedes, which with its heavier componentry and good track record of PSV service was a more rugged, reliable vehicle altogether — if not quite so pretty.

Already Optare's midibuses were beginning to affect other designs; the MCW Metrorider had a similar profile, and builders such as Northern Counties and Wright offered more stylish front ends to disguise the van-like style of their vehicles. Ironically the latter didn't catch on, but, when Optare offered a standard Mercedes cowl for the front of a lower-cost version of the StarRider, that failed to attract buyers either. Again, the StarRider particularly appealed in London, where 123 entered service. Both the CityPacer and StarRider were exported too, in left-hand-drive form. There weren't large numbers of these, but two CityPacers and 10 StarRiders went to the Netherlands, and three StarRiders were exported to Luxembourg.

Optare was well and truly established as a midibus builder, but it was soon to diversify into larger buses. The first hint came in 1987, when West Yorkshire PTE was still pursuing its dream of reintroducing trolleybuses to Bradford, and an

Below: **Also popular in London and a rather more solid, reliable vehicle than the CityPacer — if not quite so stylish — was the StarRider.** *R. J. Waterhouse*

artist's impression was released showing a dual-door single-deck trolleybus with CityPacer-style front end. Optare never did build a trolleybus but the following year unveiled its first full-size design — the Delta, based on DAF SB220 chassis — which bore a striking resemblance to that trolleybus design.

The Delta body was aluminium-built, Optare having entered into a licensing agreement with Alusuisse, which provided its bolted aluminium framing. (Thus far Wright had been the UK's only licence-holder with Alusuisse.) It was a tried and tested system which had the advantage that Optare could concentrate on styling and finishing, the Alusuisse framing coming with a proven record for structural strength.

The SB220 was a new chassis to the UK, a full-size rear-engined chassis from a builder hitherto known here only for coaches, yet the Delta quickly carved a niche for itself in a sector of the market that was particularly difficult — already the market was polarising between midibuses and double-deckers. What market existed was dominated by the Leyland Lynx, which overnight looked decidedly utilitarian against the sleek newcomer.

The Delta was launched at the 1988 Motor Show, and at the time someone who shall remain nameless described it in *Buses* as the Star of the Show. That someone obviously hadn't got his 20/20-hindsight glasses on, because at the same show was a newcomer in the single-deck market that would put everything in the shade. Dennis was launching its Dart midibus, which bridged the gap

between minibuses and full-size single-deckers, and suddenly midibuses were the sector of the market to be in. Dennis stole an amazing march on its rivals which left even mighty Volvo struggling to keep up. Optare duly cast around for a suitable chassis partner, which it found in MAN, which had a similar-sized chassis, the 11.190, and the Delta body was suitably scaled down and fitted to the MAN as the Vecta.

The Vecta was never going to take a huge proportion of the market, but it offered a segmentation of the midibus market. The Dart was in many ways a grown-up minibus; at first its target was the 25-30-seat sector dominated by Mercedes, its components being lightweight and straight-forward. The Vecta was bigger, being a 40-seater built to a full 2.5m width, and had 'big bus' components such as a ZF gearbox and air suspension. Here was a competitor for the Dart that came from the opposite end of the spectrum.

By now Optare had become well and truly established as a major player in the business. It was, it's true, something of a niche builder; in the main years of its production, 1989-93, the Delta averaged around 65 a year, but it brought Optare into some major operators which had not previously taken its products, such as Trent, Northumbria, PMT and United. Reading Buses, which had recently had 10 Olympians bodied by Optare, was one of the first Delta customers. The styling of the Delta also appealed to airlines and airport operators, such that British Airways bought 45 and several others were used on car-park work at airports.

The parlous state of the British bus-manufacturing industry had still not improved, however, and at the end of 1988 the Laird Group, having been prevented by the Government from buying Leyland to create a viable large-scale British bus manufacturer, decided the time had come to pull out and sell its Metro-Cammell-Weymann subsidiary, which was then building around 600 vehicles a year. A buyer for the business was not forthcoming, but Optare agreed to buy the Metrorider design and production. The Metrocab taxi business went to specialist car builder Reliant, and at the time it looked as if a joint venture between Plaxton and Iveco would take on the Metrobus.

Optare quickly set about reworking the Metrorider, not least to rid it of its reputation for corrosion, and in so doing adopted some of the techniques employed in the StarRider. Stretched-steel side panels were replaced with conventional aluminium panelling, while the skirt copied that of the

StarRider. The range was rationalised, the six-cylinder Cummins B-series driving through Allison transmission being the only combination offered; this had been far and away the most popular option for the MCW Metrorider, though Perkins and four-cylinder Cummins engines had been offered, as had a manual gearbox. With its customary speed, Optare, having taken on the Metrorider designs in the summer of 1989, had the first Optare MetroRider ready for that autumn's Motor Show, with a subtle name change to make it a sister to the StarRider in the Optare range. The first was a bus for Ipswich, though that remained something of a one-off, as a Mk 2 version was immediately developed with gasket (rather than bonded) glazing and a stronger rear-end structure.

The MetroRider gave Optare some real volume at last, and well over 1,000 would be built over the following 10 years. By the end of its life it had reached a Mk 4 version, with a lower floorline to meet the DiPTAC requirements of the time. It was also built in Malaysia by DRB, Malaysia's largest automotive manufacturer and distribution business, and a programme to update public transport in the

Below: **Optare's move into the big-time came with its acquisition of the rights to the Metrorider from MCW, which was withdrawing from the industry.** *Optare*

Right: **Optare had always been keen on breaking into export; through United Bus this dual-door left-hand-drive MetroRider was offered by DAF Bus on the Norwegian market.** *Optare*

capital, Kuala Lumpur, involved 1,200 examples of the PekanRider, the locally built version of the MetroRider.

Plaxton and Iveco's joint bid for the Metrobus got nowhere, and soon after acquiring the rights to the Metrorider, Optare, jointly with DAF, also acquired the rights to the Metrobus, including those to the Metroliner range of coaches, although that was dead and buried and would not be exhumed, despite some consideration being given to reviving MCW's last design, the 4m-high 400GT double-decker. Whereas Metrorider production continued almost without a break, a more considered view would be taken of the Metrobus, particularly in view of a desire to replace its all-steel structure with Alusuisse, which would be the first use of this system for a double-decker.

In the meantime the tie-up with DAF was strengthened further. There were a number of smaller, niche manufacturers throughout Europe and they saw their strength in combining their interests. This began in November 1989, when DAF and Bova, which already used DAF components in its integral coaches, together formed United Bus. DAF was the majority shareholder, and its bus and coach interests were separated from its truck production, a new Dutch headquarters being established in Eindhoven. It had aspirations towards developing subsidiary companies in most European countries, and Optare joined the group in May 1990. Russell Richardson became UK Chief Executive of United Bus, and DAF Bus UK moved out of its parent company's headquarters into Optare's Cross Gates

factory in Leeds. Russell Richardson also became DAF Bus UK's Managing Director.

United Bus never did achieve its goal of becoming a pan-European organisation, but later in 1990 Danish company DAB (a former Leyland subsidiary) joined, to be followed by another Dutch company, bodybuilder Den Oudsten. DAF's share in the business was reduced from 56% to 35% with increased involvement from Dutch banks.

Meanwhile DAF was developing a new underframe to replace the Metrobus. Not a great deal of the original Metrobus concept was going to remain in the new vehicle: DAF used the front end of the SB220 chassis and fitted a transverse rear engine of its own, with only the GKN hub-reduction rear axle and MCW's H-beam rear suspension being carried over. The Metrobus had always used a Voith gearbox, which was also carried over, but ZF became an option too. Optare's bodywork was completely new, owing more to the Delta than the Metrobus, and once again the styling left other builders behind, with deep curved screens on both decks, although its overall profile owed more than a little to the Metrobus. It was the first new double-deck design for 10 years and provoked both Alexander and Northern Counties to develop upmarket versions of their standard bodies, which had looked dated as soon as the Spectra, as Optare christened its new double-decker, was launched at Coach & Bus '91 show.

The engine in the Spectra was kept a closely guarded secret, but turned out to be a brand-new RS-series 8.65-litre unit which had been developed by DAF as a replacement for the Leyland-derived 11.6-litre units in its truck range, in readiness for the ever-tightening emissions regulations then coming into force; as it made no sense to develop the new chassis with the old engine, the RS range was fitted to the Spectra even though it had not yet been announced to the truck world. Reading, by now a loyal Optare customer and a previous user of Metrobuses, took the first three, while Wilts & Dorset, already a MetroRider customer, was to become the most significant buyer of the type.

The United Bus era proved remarkably brief and, far from giving Optare greater strength, almost proved its undoing. While Optare was used to rocky markets, having been conceived and born at the worst possible time for Britain's buses, the Dutch companies in particular were used to a steady market with plenty of state funding. However, in the early 1990s the Dutch market collapsed, and with United Bus's strong dependence on the Netherlands the company fell into receivership in 1993. Russell Richardson duly succeeded in buying back Optare from the receivers and established a new Optare Holdings company.

United Bus had required member companies to use DAF where appropriate, and diversification from products depending on DAF chassis became a priority. Dennis's Lance enabled Optare to offer a lighter-weight, lower-cost full-size single-decker, and, in the only instance of collaboration between

Above: **Undoubtedly the star of Coach & Bus '91 was the Spectra, Britain's first new double-decker for a decade.** *Stephen Morris*

Below: **After the failure of United Bus Optare sought new chassis partners, and the first result was the Dennis Lance-based Sigma. This is one of 20 delivered to Brighton & Hove.** *Stephen Morris*

Right: **The first Prisma at its launch at Mercedes' Milton Keynes headquarters. 'Someone' amongst the assembled journalists found that the destination blind was obviously intended to be moved from vehicle to vehicle and could also show 'DAF SB220' and 'Dennis Lance'; it was duly photographed thus until someone from Mercedes caught us and there were ructions! To take the heat out of the situation I promised to forward all my negs and prints of the Prisma showing a rival chassis on its destination blind, so I can't show you one, sadly. There are times when principles are a bit of a nuisance!** *Stephen Morris*

Left: **Optare maintained its styling flair when it introduced its first low-floor model, the all-steel integral Excel, seen here at its launch in 1995.** *Stephen Morris*

Dennis and Optare, the Alusuisse single-deck body, with the Vecta's less distinctive front end, was offered on the Lance as the Sigma. It was hardly a great success: just 53 were sold in a two-year period, most of them to Go-Ahead Northern, Trent and Brighton & Hove, and, although Trent cascaded them to its Notts & Derby subsidiary and then to driver training as soon as possible, Brighton & Hove is still pleased with its batch of 20, which remain on front-line work. Optare went on to collaborate with Mercedes-Benz, bodying the O.405 chassis as the Prisma with Mercedes' own front end.

The Prisma for the first time established Mercedes as a supplier of large buses to the UK market. It was also bought by companies in the growing GRT group — Grampian, Leicester Citybus and SMT — which were trying to push up the quality of their new vehicles and took Prismas with air-conditioning and double-glazing and also took similar buses from Wright, on the O.405 and Scania N113. North East Bus, then owned by West Midlands Travel, also took 25 for its Tees & District company. By the time the Prisma had been launched, however, the world was moving on to low-floor buses. Optare decided it would build on its experience of integral construction with the MetroRider and do its own thing. Almost overnight Optare ceased to be a bodybuilder (Spectra aside) and became a manufacturer of complete vehicles.

Once again Dennis had stolen a march by developing a low-floor version of the Dart, and all of a sudden low-floor buses ceased to be an expensive toy and became the mainstream; had Optare persisted with the Prisma as its main single-decker it would very quickly have found no-one would buy it because it had steps. Again the Dart became the benchmark at which to aim, and the Excel, as Optare's new low-floor single-decker was named, shared a similar style of all-steel construction to the MetroRider; like the MetroRider and the Dart, it was powered by the six-cylinder Cummins B-series, albeit the most powerful, 220bhp version, which meant going up to the heavier-duty and altogether more sophisticated Allison World Series transmission. Optare found that building the vehicle in its entirety brought significant cost savings over buying-in chassis and that building the complete structure and fitting the mechanical units as a package at the last minute also brought significant cash-flow benefits.

The Excel, though pitched in the same market sector as the Dart SLF, had several factors the Dart didn't: true to Optare's form, there was nothing then on the market to touch it in styling terms — typically, though not exclusively, the Dart came with Plaxton's rather uninspired Pointer, which even after a facelift was never going to turn heads — and again Optare went for a 'big bus' approach, with full width and full-sized wheels, which gave it some disadvantage in terms of internal layout but addressed issues facing Dart operators over braking. Besides this, Optare's designers were able to produce a particularly attractive interior despite greater intrusion from the wheel arches.

It would be nice to be able to say that the Excel took the world by storm; indeed, at first it seemed it was doing well. However, many operators found the Dart a more practical proposition, and I spent a day

Right: **Fylde Borough Transport, by then owned by neighbouring Blackpool, was the first customer for the Excel. It counted the type as a midibus and thus painted its examples in yellow Handybus livery. These proved short-lived with Fylde, being replaced by a new batch, and have since found new owners.**
Stephen Morris

Left: **Leicester Citybus took a small batch of Excels, which were used to launch First's new interior.** *Stephen Morris*

Right: **Optare was optimistic that the Excel would gain a sizeable proportion of orders placed to update Malta's bus fleet, and this example, exported in 1997, was expected to be the first of many. It remains a one-off.**
Stephen Morris

Left: **The Spectra was reworked as a low-floor bus; this impressive vehicle for Sargeant's of Kington is by far the most modern double-decker in Herefordshire.**
Optare

Right: **A recent low-floor Spectra is this dual-door vehicle supplied to the Armed Forces as a bare shell for fitting-out as an elaborate recruitment unit.**
Stephen Morris

Left: **The Solo got off to a good start thanks to an order for 85 from Wilts & Dorset.** *Stephen Morris*

Below: **The Solo has proved popular with a wide range of customers and has become virtually the standard low-floor small bus for First.** *Optare*

with Brian King of Trent, which had bought both, in which he sought to convince me that the practicality of the Dart outweighed the 'wow factor' of the Excel. He was probably right but went on to buy large quantities of Excels and repented at leisure, selling them early and replacing them with Scanias.

Maybe the Excel was a step too far, but Optare persisted with building its own complete vehicles. It had on the stocks designs for a new low-floor minibus, which had the potential to take the world by storm. DAF had been at the forefront of low-floor double-deckers, with a lowered-frame version of its DB250 — the Spectra's chassis by now being available to other bodybuilders — and Optare managed to get the first new-generation low-floor double-deckers on the road. The smart, modern

appearance of the Spectra meant it didn't have to start from scratch to produce a new generation for a new era and was able to adapt its existing double-decker for low-floor. But the one thing that no-one had yet tackled effectively was the low-floor minibus.

Russell Richardson was hesitant to commit to production, but Wilts & Dorset was desperate to have a low-floor replacement for its huge Metrorider fleet and forced his hand by promising to order 85 off the drawing board. Construction was broadly similar to the Excel, and the driveline from the Mercedes Vario was used, mounted at the rear of the bus. Having no front overhang, with the entrance just behind the front wheels, meant that approach angles were not a problem, and the new minibus, named Solo, was thus able to feature a lower entrance than could any conventional low-floor bus. It wasn't exactly 'mini' perhaps; Wilts & Dorset specified the full 2.5m width, and it was made available in 8.5 and 9m lengths, but, despite Russell Richardson's reservations as to whether it would sell, it became hugely popular. Whereas Optare's 'niche' products meant it had built up a rather narrow customer base of medium-sized operators like Trent, Go-Ahead, Wilts & Dorset and Reading Buses, which saw the benefits of buses which stood out from the crowd and could afford to pay for them, the Solo launched Optare into a different league, with all the major groups buying it, while a tie-up with dealer Mistral, which offered attractive rental packages, made it accessible to smaller operators too. And more than one county council bought the type to lease to operators to provide accessible buses on tendered rural services. The Solo was the only bus to gain a Prime Minister's Millennium Award for innovation, and styling-wise it was almost a 21st-century equivalent of the CityPacer. During 2004 the first narrow versions were due to enter service, to overcome the resistance to a 2.5m-wide vehicle in this class, and a Cummins engine option was offered.

Having broken into the larger minibuses, Optare faced its next challenge in producing something for the true minibus market, and its next product was even more innovative. The Alero was the first fully accessible true minibus and again broke the mould. Styling this time was based very firmly on the 'people carrier' concept — it has overtones of the Toyota Previa, in particular — with the idea of making a bus which no longer looked like a bus. In

a way it reverted to the original concept of the grand-daddy of all low-floor buses, the prototype Bristol Lodekka, by putting the propshaft along the side of the bus to allow a full-length step-free gangway and used a front-mounted Iveco engine and an unusual one-piece composite construction. The Alero, with its innovative approach, took some time to get into production and suffered a few teething troubles but overcame its initial difficulties. It coincided with Government grants for innovative rural services and a new interest in demand-responsive transport for rural areas and, like earlier Optare products, has carved out a significant niche for itself. Now Optare is studying ways of adapting it for other uses as an all-purpose community vehicle with the major advantage over truck-based vehicles of easy accessibility.

Optare had also been importing coach bodywork from Spain on a Mercedes truck chassis as well as smaller coaches on the Ford Transit, finishing them in this country and marketing them as its own products through Optare Coach Sales, diversification into the smaller coaches having begun in 1996 when it bought Rotherham-based Autobus Classique, which built stylish midicoach bodies on Mercedes chassis.

In early 2000 Optare finally conceded that its future was not as an independent company and agreed to sell to NABI — North American Bus Industries. Despite its name NABI is a Hungarian firm set up to continue the North American operations of Ikarus and is owned largely by a Jersey-based venture-capital fund which invests in Hungarian industry.

Right: **Optare's true mini, the Alero, has found a niche for demand-responsive services. This one is used by Arriva in Bedfordshire.** *John Smith*

Throughout its existence Optare has been keen on breaking into exports, and its first major success was introducing double-deckers to Turkey, with 31 Spectras — followed, of course, by the 1,200 Malaysian PekanRiders. NABI has given Optare access to the US market through the Model 30-LFN, which you and I would recognise as the Solo, and in 2003 the Solo and Alero were launched into Europe at the Kortrijk show in the Netherlands.

The question that everyone keeps asking is: 'When will Optare's new double-decker appear?' It has been a badly kept secret that Optare is working on a highly innovative new integral double-decker which would even suit London's requirements for a rear-entrance Routemaster replacement. However, it appears that London no longer wants such a beast, and with huge investment already having been put into double-deckers for London it seems that Optare may have missed the bus, as it were.

In its 20 years Optare has had a sometimes turbulent existence, but the rate of its progress, from an empty factory in Leeds through box-like buses, ambulances and welfare buses and building Leyland-style bodies on Olympians to a reputation for style and innovation, has been nothing short of remarkable.

HOME *FIXTURES*

Billy Nicol visits the streets around Ibrox Stadium, home of Glasgow Rangers Football Club, to photograph the vehicles transporting visiting fans to home games.

Above: A varied line-up of a dozen coaches, headed by a Bova Futura from the fleet of Maynes of Buckie.

Right: This is a rare beast, a 1989 Leyland Swift with Wadham Stringer body. It started life as a demonstrator and reached the fleet of Stuarts of Carluke via Tayside Police.

Above left: **Golden Eagle is the trading name of long-established operator Irvine of Salsburgh. This Leyland Tiger joined the Golden Eagle fleet in 2000. It has a Duple Caribbean body and was new in 1984 to Southend Transport.**

Above: **Another Golden Eagle Leyland is this Leopard with Plaxton Supreme IV body, one of three purchased from Cleveland Transit in 1995. It is seen at Ibrox in 2001.**

Above: **Irvine of Law operates this Atlantean with Willowbrook body which was rebuilt as a coach by Merseyside Transport in 1991. It was new in 1981.**

Right: **Jay Coaches of Coatbridge operates a number of Dennis Dominators with Alexander R-type bodies which were new to South Yorkshire PTE.**

Right: Only two Alexander TC-type bodies were supplied new to independent operators, but a number of used examples can now be seen running for smaller fleets. This 1985 TC, on a Leyland Tiger chassis, was new to Fife Scottish but now runs for Docherty of Irvine.

Left: Marshall's of Baillieston operates this smart East Lancs-bodied Volvo Citybus, built as a demonstrator. It was bought by A1 of Ardrossan and passed to Stagecoach when A1 was taken over. Marshall's bought it in 2000.

Right: New to Glen Coaches of Port Glasgow in 2001 was this Iveco EuroRider with Beulas Stergo E body. It is seen at Ibrox soon after entering service.